UNDAUNTED
STORIES OF FREEDOM IN
A SHACKLED SOCIETY

GABRIEL DOLAN

**FOREWORD BY
MAINA KIAI**

AUGUST 2021

Published by
Zand Graphics Ltd
P O Box 32843-00600
Tel: 0722 344900 / 0787 557454
Nairobi, Kenya

Editorial Management: Zarina Patel
Cover design: One Media
Cover cartoon: Gado

THE OPEN SOCIETY INITIATIVE
FOR EASTERN AFRICA

The publication of this memoir was supported by the Open Society Initiative for Eastern Africa (OSIEA). The views in this memoir are the author's and not those of OSIEA.

ISBN: 978-9914-40-249-0

Zand Graphics Ltd is an independent publishing company specialising in print publication. We provide a complete turnkey service from editing to design and print production. We believe in providing a product with the client's core business in mind at a competitive and fair price, with guaranteed reliability.

Visit **www.zandgraphics.com** for more information about us and purchase of our books.

TABLE OF CONTENTS

✚

ACKNOWLEDGEMENTS

Writing may be a passion but it also requires discipline, patience and human support. I deeply appreciate the many people who have encouraged me to put my thoughts and experiences on paper and the many others who assisted along the way to its eventual publication. For several years, colleagues like Willy Mutunga, Maina Kiai, Ling Kituyi, Peter Kiama and many others prompted me to take up the challenge. For long I hesitated and then eventually put hands to the keyboard when my travels and commitments were restricted by the pandemic.

Thanks to Tim Redmond for his professional, gentle and supportive editing. He convinced me that I had a story to tell. There was also constant support from John Marren and Willie Walsh who kept me motivated in a variety of ways. I will be eternally grateful to the ever enthusiastic and courageous Zahid Rajan and Zarina Patel of Zand Graphics who came to the rescue when church publishers found the document too hot to handle. Their belief in the value of the contents got me to the next stage. Thanks too to Gado for the use of his cartoon on the front cover.

My sincerest gratitude goes to George Kegoro and the wonderful staff at Open Society of East Africa (OSIEA) who have funded the publication and launch and eventually made all of this become a reality. The constant inspiration and insight I receive from my Haki Yetu family is a great boost. While my blood family - Dolans Worldwide - keep me grounded and prevent me from getting carried away. I dedicate this to all of you. Any small contributions received from the distribution of the books will be shared by two wonderful ladies – Esther in Likoni, Mombasa and Mary in Mtopeni, Mtwapa – whose work for Spinabifidal children in the two centers constantly reminds me of the rights and needs of the most vulnerable of our citizens. God bless them all.

FOREWORD

I am humbled and honoured to have been asked to write this foreword to Father Gabriel Dolan's short memoirs.

I have known Father Gabriel since the mid-1990s when we met in Lodwar when I was part of an evaluation exercise to see how to strengthen the Catholic Justice and Peace Commission of Lodwar. It was a life-changing experience for me, not only because Father Gabriel introduced me one evening to the delights of Irish Whiskey, but also because he became one of my closest friends and a person I admire and look up to for his humility, fortitude and consistency.

In simple terms, Father Gabriel is a believer in Christ, and significantly embodies what a real Christian should be. I just wish that more of our religious leaders were as true to the Word as he is.

These memoirs should be compulsory reading for everyone interested in social justice and change. They trace Kenya's history since the 1980s in simple, readable, and exciting ways, reminding us that though we have come a long way from the 1980s, we are really not out of the woods and we could easily slide back to those dark days if we do not remain vigilant, clear headed and focused on the ideals, rather than on the personalities.

From his work in Turkana, Kitale, Kapenguria and Mombasa, Father Gabriel reminds us that true transformative change comes from the people themselves, from the bottom up. This is a challenge that the social justice/human rights practitioners must internalize and the sooner the better. The idea of being the "voice of the voiceless" must transform to facilitating, encouraging and giving space to those who suffer the indignities of injustice, violence, poverty and repression. Indeed, one of the most significant tasks for the human rights community is to devolve away from Nairobi, in real, practical, and substantive ways.

Especially urgent is the need for the human rights sector to eschew the practice that some have copied from the political class of financial "facilitation" fees to encourage participation in activities aimed at addressing or mitigating the problems that afflict the majority in this country. Human rights must not be transactional, and those of us involved in this work must be there for the long-term with all the attendant frustrations.

Human rights work has its lonely moments and being part of a community is crucial for mental stability and focus. It is by no means accidental that Father Gabriel's background as a Catholic priest and the community that that provides has been a significant factor in his longevity and success. Yet as he reminds us, the Church itself can be an obstacle when it too becomes a part of the ruling class and focuses more on status, access to power and privilege rather than be the catalyst for transformative change that Jesus embodied.

Sometimes the struggles for change are made bigger, and harder, because of the international hierarchy of power. Many think that the last four years of the Trump regime epitomized the disconnect between rhetoric and action of the US and its approach to human rights, but as far back as 2000, the US was playing fast and loose with facts and truth regarding the assassination of Father Kaiser for its own "strategic" interests, when the FBI was called in to "investigate" the killing. That the US could so callously play with the truth around the killing of its own (white) citizen in Father Kaiser's assassination speaks volumes about its real views of human rights domestically and internationally.

The struggle for change in Kenya is a long-term struggle but many of us thought we had turned the corner with the end of KANU as the ruling party. But we forgot how deeply entrenched Moism and KANUISM were as the new ruling class proceeded simply to replace some of the Moi era actors with new ones steeped in the same predatory values of primitive accumulation and self-service.

That process was cemented in 2013 when people indicted for crimes against humanity were imposed on us in the top leadership of the country. The flouting of the new constitution to allow the indicted persons to contest for high office signaled the consolidation of impunity, corruption, violence, and division in Kenya. It is not surprising, hence, that we have been on a downward spiral since.

I would hazard a guess that Father Dolan's longevity and drive, is as much due to his spiritual strength, as it is because he has had changes of locations for his work, from Turkana to Kitale to Kapenguria to Mombasa, as well as different focuses in his work. The fact that he has had sabbaticals and time away to reflect and study cannot be gainsaid. If human rights defenders are to maintain their tempo, their drive and avoid burn out, sabbaticals, time away from the work studying and writing, as well not doing the same thing year on, year out, need to be instituted. And we must celebrate our victories, lavishly and loudly so, even if these are few and far between. Similarly, we need to celebrate the pioneers, those who have inspired us, and focused us so that the new generation of activists know how far we have come.

It is not easy for a white man, with all the attendant privileges that brings, to become an integral part of the struggle for pro-poor transformative change in Kenya, and be subject to arrest, harassment, and repression. Yet, that white privilege, and indeed other privileges, can also be used positively to protect others, shine a light on violations and repression and facilitate this long struggle that will not end. This is something that is consciously done, and Father Gabriel has played his role magnificently.

For those who read these memoirs, please circulate them to everyone you know. Translate them, read them in the mosques, churches and under trees so that Kenyans can get a sense of where we have come from, what we should avoid, and what it takes to make some gains that benefit the majority of our people.

Maina Kiai

Nairobi, February 2021

INTRODUCTION

The failed coup d'état attempt of 1 August 1982 shocked political analysts who never imagined that Kenya would travel the route of their West African cousins in trusting the military to do a better job at governance than a civilian administration. However, within twenty-four hours the threat was overcome, the insurgents detained and the Moi government had regained control. There followed a vicious purge of real and imaginary enemies and the arrest of the alleged coup plotters and just about everyone else considered a threat to the floundering KANU regime of President Daniel arap Moi.

Six weeks later I made my maiden trip to Kenya arriving at a tense and nervous Jomo Kenyatta International Airport to be received by hordes of heavily armed General Service Unit (GSU) soldiers with a supporting cast of Israeli troops that made little effort to hide their identity or interest. There goes my naive image, I thought, of Kenya as a haven of peace renowned for its hospitality, game parks and sandy beaches. Yet, far from being intimidated or anxious I managed a wry smile and thought to myself 'out of the frying pan and into the fire'. This was a real déjà vu experience. Fifteen hours earlier I had left a similar scene in Belfast Airport where strategic government facilities received the same heavy-duty security from the British Army.

A few days later I was driven to Turkana to take up my first missionary appointment in the Catholic Diocese of Lodwar. It was a daunting experience to arrive in a harsh, empty, arid land where only the toughest and most resilient appeared to survive. Having never experienced such hot temperatures, poverty and remoteness I wondered what God intended me to undertake in such a challenging and hostile environment.

The following Sunday I went for Mass at St Augustine's Church in Lodwar town. The service was led by Bishop John Mahon and the church was filled with joyful worshippers. However, the whole mood of the service changed when the Bishop stood and read the Pastoral Letter that the Kenyan Bishops Conference had recently scripted in response to the attempted coup. It mainly focused on the need to live peacefully as a nation and retain respect for the rule of law and for dialogue. It was not hard-hitting, more like a gentle slap on the wrist to the besieged government and a pious admonition to Kenyans to live in harmony and move forward as one united nation.

The congregation listened intently and presumed that was it until the prelate straightened himself up, adjusted the microphone, raised his voice and began to address the issues and realities that he considered had been overlooked in the Bishops' pastoral letter. You could have heard a pin drop as the faithful began to nervously digest what he was saying. He concluded by warning that further coups and revolts might well take place if Kenyans were to continue to be denied their political and social freedoms and the twin cancers of corruption and tribalism were left unaddressed. This was provocative and courageous preaching like I had never witnessed before.

Mass ended; the congregation trooped home discussing the contents of his homily in quiet whispers. Bishop Mahon joined us in the parish house for his usual cup of tea but soon we were interrupted by loud knocking on the door by three burly gentlemen who quickly identified themselves as national security personnel. They entered before being invited and immediately asked the Bishop for a copy of his homily. He replied that he had not carried one but since he had recognised them in the congregation they already had heard and probably recorded what he preached. He then duly informed them that he stood by what he had said and had no regret or apology for his words, 'What I have said, I have said, I will not retract, that is all I have to say to you'.

The special branch men were stunned into silence and exited meekly, most likely to return to their security office and write a report for the regular Monday morning provincial security briefing with their superiors in Nakuru. With Moi's elaborate intelligence machinery reporting every alleged dissident and threat to the nation's security, no doubt that report had reached his desk in State House by midday Monday.

That did not bother John Mahon and it delighted me. The eight years of study were over, the hands-on experience was underway, and I was appointed to work with a leader who would inspire, confront and witness to a life of simplicity, humility, service and justice. This was why I wanted to be a missionary, I thought to myself. This was the launching pad to my ministry for justice, peace and radical change.

Four decades later, the transformation of Kenya into a democratic, just and accountable society is far from complete. The country has made modest political, social and economic progress since 1982. Yet successive regimes have failed miserably to address the needs, dreams and aspirations of the forty-seven million citizens. The crimes that John Mahon raged about in that hot, dusty pulpit in Lodwar forty years ago are as pervasive today as they were then. Corruption has become the national pastime of the ruling class while Kenya remains one of the most unequal and divided societies on the planet.

The reformers of four decades ago have mostly followed John Mahon to their graves as sad, impoverished, burned out and forgotten individuals. The country's wealth is still in the hands of a few dynastic families and the nation's slums expand on a daily basis. Few would have dared to predict that Kenyans would by 2020 still be held hostage by a corrupt, elitist leadership and a police force that tortures, harasses and eliminates its citizens as a matter of routine.

Yet this feeble effort at sharing my experiences and encounters is not intended to bring despair but to inspire and provoke. There is a lot of good news to arouse hope for the future. There are very many great people who still believe in 'project Kenya', willing to defend the weak and demanding to be heard in their quest for a better life for their children. Most of the stories told here are about these ordinary brave and heroic individuals who retain a passion for justice and resolutely resist oppression and bad governance with energy and commitment. They merit recognition and honour and I hope that I have done them justice.

These ramblings are also intended for the younger generation, those who never experienced the brutality and oppression of the Moi regime and are not familiar with the history of struggle in Kenya. The aim is to reflect on the lessons learned and acknowledge the mistakes made so that the next generation of human rights advocates and activists can benefit as they prepare to take their place in leading Kenya and its institutions into a better space.

I hope that readers can also experience some of the joy that I have encountered in this great missionary venture and that they retain vision, happiness and love for all of God's humanity and creation. Whatever failures and disappointments may result from our efforts we must never lose the joy and inner satisfaction of doing what is right, regardless of the outcome. There is no room for resentment, regrets, bitterness or constant anger in a ministry of justice and peace. The hardships only refine and purify our motivation and we must continue to smile knowing that 'the arc of moral justice is long but it bends towards justice', as Martin Luther King Jr said more than half a century ago.

This publication is divided into two sections. The first half is devoted to sharing significant experiences, incidents and reflections from my time in Turkana, Kitale and Mombasa since 1982 until today. The second part is a selection of my weekly Op-Ed columns for the Daily Nation and East African Standard during the period 2008-20. They are just a small selection of the 500 plus columns that I submitted during that time. I have chosen those that appear to have passed the test of time and others that provoked the most reaction and debate – not always positive - when first published.

I have entitled this book, **Undaunted – Stories of Freedom in a Shackled Society.** We were born free and with our eyes open. God destined us to live as free, joyful people summed up in the words of Jesus who said, *'I came that you may have life, life in all its fullness'* (John 10:10). That life should be one that is free from poverty, oppression, ignorance, violence and discrimination. The fullness of life makes us free from superstition, worry and negativity. The longing to be free is a noble lifelong venture yet the only one befitting our human nature.

But to free oneself or assist in liberating others involves taking risks, being suspicious of the status quo, leaving the safety of the shore and launching out into the deep and the unknown. This is a very lonely calling too as one immerses oneself into the whole of reality with courage to confront and listen. Yet, the calling is not to be the liberator of the oppressed but to make a commitment to fight alongside them, as Paulo Freire wrote in Pedagogy of the Oppressed.[1]

Yet that journey of liberation is also fraught with doubts, failures and fears, but that is understandable since the struggle for liberation is much greater than our knowledge and experience of it. Indeed, acknowledging that truth is both liberating and humbling in itself. Work for justice endures when we share a deep faith in the God who liberates the downtrodden. Faith in God requires that we also trust his people's ability to articulate their oppression and identify their needs while encouraging them to mobilise for the change that they yearn for.

My good friend and constant inspiration, Maina Kiai, has very kindly agreed to

---

1   Paulo Freire, Pedagogy of the Oppressed, p 19

write the foreword. We have shared many struggles over the last twenty-five years, walked together in protests all over Kenya and shared many boardrooms and bars. He remains an inspiration, a global giant in the field of human rights through his work with Kenya Human Rights Commission, Amnesty International, Kenyan National Commission for Human Rights, Inform Action, Muhuri, Human Rights Watch and most recently as a board member of Facebook's online monitoring content project.

I dedicate this book to the many Kenyan women and men, young and old from all walks of life that I have been blessed to work alongside for four decades in this work of justice and transformation. These heroines and heroes are too many to mention by name but I salute all of you and am honoured to have known you. The following poem by the late Mary Oliver is to honour all who are truly 'untamed, undaunted, wild geese' and have given their lives and energy to a noble and great adventure:

Wild Geese
You do not have to be good.
You do not have to walk on your knees
for a hundred miles through the desert repenting.
You only have to let the soft animal of your body
love what it loves.
Tell me about despair, yours, and I will tell you mine.
Meanwhile the world goes on.
Meanwhile the sun and the clear pebbles of the rain
are moving across the landscapes,
over the prairies and the deep trees,
the mountains and the rivers.
Meanwhile the wild geese, high in the clean blue air,
are heading home again.
Whoever you are, no matter how lonely,
the world offers itself to your imagination,
calls to you like the wild geese, harsh and exciting -
over and over announcing your place
in the family of things.

1

RAW BEGINNINGS IN THE DESERT

There is no secret formula for human rights work. There are skills and strategies that can be learned and shared, but what drives most people committed to the work of peace and justice is passion. That cannot be acquired in the classroom or in textbooks; it is either in your blood and calling or it is not. Human Rights work can never be a job even if it does put bread on the table for your family. Its demands go far beyond normal working hours and the passionate figure seeking for genuine change is ever restless, always wanting to defend the poor and the persecuted.

In the mission of Jesus, the calling is to comfort the afflicted and afflict the comfortable; to heal and to disturb the peace of those who imagine that all is well. In the words of the man from Galilee again, once you put your hand to the plough there is no going back.[2] Once you identify with this mission and vocation you are in it for keeps; you are hooked. Those who seek acclaim, profit or recognition for this work rarely last the pace and eventually move out and on to the realms of law, politics, journalism and business. The greatest reward for those who respond to this calling is the satisfaction of witnessing positive change even if only after many years of struggle.

There are many ways and opportunities to uplift the community and promote change wherever we are. My early experiences in Turkana were of teaching in the classrooms of Lodwar High School in the early 1980s and of helping to build primary schools with the hope that the next generation would get a better opportunity to pursue their dreams and develop their God given talents. Being young and energetic and with lots of crazy ideas, together with a colleague, John Marren, we started a youth centre in Lodwar town in 1986. Lokiriama was a meeting hall, games centre and the first public library in Turkana District. It gave space, light and a comfortable learning environment to hundreds of youths on a daily basis. It is still going strong after 35 years.

As the numbers grew and the interests of the youth expanded, I was asked to become Youth Coordinator for the Diocese of Lodwar in 1989 by that visionary,

---

2   Luke 9:62

wise and extraordinarily humble Bishop, John Mahon. Training of leaders began in schools and parishes, in classrooms and under the trees. Ably assisted by Davis Wafula and Willimena Asekon, we also held annual sports, drama and music festivals for the youth of the vast Turkana District.

As literacy improved and leaders emerged, we decided that there was a real need to have a publication that would give a voice to the youth to share their experiences and their views. A very simple publication emerged called in Kiswahili *Sauti ya Jamii* (The Voice of the People). At its initial stage it just shared news, then it began to receive views and later the youth started writing about injustices, leadership and corruption in their own locality. Printed on unreliable second-hand photocopiers it began with a print run of 100 copies. By the early 1990s the quarterly run was 1,000 copies selling at ten shillings per copy (equivalent to a few cents of a Euro).

The magazine did not require registration, nor would it have been granted a licence in those turbulent times. Bear in mind that Turkana was still a formally closed area and the only political party that was known and permitted was KANU right up until 1997, despite the fact that Kenya had become a multi-party democracy in 1990.

For the first time since independence the provincial administration was being asked to account for their behaviour to those they were appointed to serve while the political class came under scrutiny from the more aware voters. Young people exposed theft and corruption in the distribution of famine relief food, in the allocation of school bursaries and in the looting of government resources. The ruling class were experiencing questioning and challenges like never before. Every copy of Sauti ya Jamii was read by at least ten people, although quite furtively, as it was deemed seditious and inflammatory by the powerful. Of course, this made it all the more enticing for the avid readers.

Politicians called for its banning, but this was not possible as it was never registered as a magazine in the first place. Japheth Ekidor, MP and Junior Minister, renamed it Sauti ya Vita (The Voice of War) and of course this added to its popularity and increased the demand for the magazine. Bishop Mahon never responded to their demands and he always received the first copy off the printer. We touched something deep in the lives of the young Turkana people and gave them a voice and cover until they were ready to find a voice of their own to express their desires and needs. We were stirring up things that had been in controlled calm water for decades.

However, sometimes the invitation to do more and be more comes in very strange and unusual circumstances as I discovered in 1993. It all began on an August evening when I was driving from Nairobi to Kitale after dropping family visitors from Ireland. As I passed Mois Bridge my vehicle was struck by an oncoming matatu (the Kiswahili word for a local taxi). I was knocked out and a few people received minor injuries. I had no doubt that I was not at fault but a corrupt policeman had other ideas.

A few months later, I received a call from an officer in Matunda police station suggesting that I might be charged with reckless driving but before proceeding with the case he would like to meet me in private. This was a typical corrupt proposition and I rejected it immediately and slammed down the telephone. Three days later a policeman in Lodwar came to the parish and issued me with a summons to appear in court in Kitale two days later to answer the charges that had already been threatened.

With a colleague, I drove the 320 kilometres and duly presented myself at the court. I tried to acquire legal representation but was duly informed that all advocates were boycotting the courts over claims of corruption and inefficiency. The charges were read and I was released on 20,000 Kenya shillings cash bail, a sizeable sum in those days. We were not prepared for such a ruling so my colleague went looking for the cash while I was hauled off to the court cells. Mindful that it was a Friday evening and that banks would close at 3pm I remained in dread amid stinking, overcrowded and dark cells.

After two hours I was called and released when the cash bail had been found and processed. It seemed like two days but what I experienced in that short time had a lasting almost Damascus-like effect on me. There were dozens of street children and petty thieves who had been there for days if not weeks. There was just one bucket – already full to the brim – for toilet purposes and no lighting nor drinking water. I emerged from the cells at around 4.30pm and insisted to my colleague, Jimmy Farrell, that we would get out of town immediately and return to Turkana.

We reached Lodwar long after midnight but next morning I woke early and drove the short distance to the home of Bishop Mahon to share with him my experiences. Over breakfast, I ended the summary by telling him that I was convinced that we must now begin a Catholic Justice and Peace Commission (CJPC) in the Diocese to give a further voice to the poor and downtrodden. Bishop John delayed his re-

17

sponse and then said words to the effect that he thought that this was not the right time to do so, but if I was ready, he would support the cause. I almost spilt the milk jug as I rushed around the table to shake his hand with delight. The foundation stone had been laid.

I spent the rest of the morning writing a proposal to Trócaire (the Irish Catholic charity which supports work for human development and social justice) for seed money as a start-up for the programme. When Kevin Carroll, the Trócaire Country Director, approved the application with some suggestions and amendments, I immediately took the next step forward and approached Peter Kiama to coordinate the programme with immediate effect.

Peter had come straight from Moi University in 1991 as a member of the Kenya Catholic Lay Missionaries (KCLM) and had been managing Lokiriama centre for three years. He had the aptitude, courage, energy and maturity to take on the responsibility. He requested a few days to think over the offer and then returned to say that he was ready for the challenge, providing that we would also employ an assistant from the local community. Peter realised how difficult it would be for a member of his own Kikuyu community (deemed opposition) to run a human rights programme in a KANU zone. So, within a few months Damian Aryong was employed to assist Peter in his new role.

As they say, the rest is history. For the record I was eventually acquitted of the driving offence after a dozen appearances in court. I had written to Attorney General Amos Wako to take remedial action against the Chief Magistrate in Kitale since I had been denied my legal right to be represented. The Magistrate was transferred, the case was heard and I was ably represented by Fatuma Sichale, currently a Court of Appeal Judge in the Kenya judiciary.

Beginnings are always difficult but few of us were expecting to be thrown in at the deep end so quickly or forced to learn on the hoof. But that was what happened at CJPC Lodwar. Within a week of our finding office space, the District Commissioner, one Reuben Rotich, began a campaign of discrimination and harassment against local businessmen who came from ethnic communities that were perceived to be opposed to the ruling party, KANU. Most of these businesspeople had no involvement at all in politics, but they were denied renewal of their business licenses and subsequently lost all their supplier's contracts. Through our lobbying and pleading on their behalf, most were granted the right to resume their businesses after a few months, but a few with less money in reserve were forced to close down and move out of Turkana.

However, when the CJPC team began programmes of civic education at parish level, the provincial administration and the administration police were unleashed to thwart our efforts and to stop all seminars. The first major incident was when police stopped a workshop for teachers in Lokitaung, in the far north of the county and the home of KANU chairman Japheth Ekidor's. Again, in Loarengak on the shores of Lake Turkana, the team were violently attacked and Peter Kiama was beaten by the local chief when the classroom was invaded. He later required medical attention.

In Kalokol town the training was held at the local Catholic church. I was in attendance with the team that day, when the chief sent two administration police to warn us not to proceed with the training. The participants, however, insisted that we continue. However, when we saw a few dozen armed riot police coming in the direction of the church one hour later, I sneaked into the sacristy and donned my liturgical vestments. As the police surrounded the church, I began the opening prayers of the Mass.

After the scripture readings, I preached for some time and then invited the team of trainers to share their input with the congregation. The police were frustrated and confused. They knew they could not by any stretch of the imagination disrupt a church service. Such news would have made national headlines and been an embarrassment to the Moi regime, even if it took place in the remote regions of Turkana County. However, the forces remained in wait and when we eventually concluded the prayer and civic education session, we had to plan our escape and exit out of the church compound.

The participants formed a human barrier between the police and the trainers. I managed to sneak out and get the pickup engine running hoping for a quick getaway. However, as I looked over my shoulder, I spotted a very burly chief lifting Kiama off the ground by virtue of a grip on his trouser belt. I charged at him and he released him. The three of us sped off into the setting sun and back to the relative security of Lodwar town.

Not all such seminars were disrupted, but it was always more challenging in the north of the county and the constituency of Japheth Ekidor. One final incident is here worth recording. In early 1997 I was due to travel to Lokitaung to visit the Young Christian Students (YCS) in the local secondary school. I had intended to travel on Friday and come back on Sunday, as Lokitaung was a five-hour journey on a very poor road. However, on Friday morning, a police friend in Lodwar passed a message to me through Peter Kiama advising me not to travel. By then I was ready to depart but after consideration I heeded his advice.

A few days later another priest of the Diocese of Lodwar, John Manzi, came to visit me. He informed me that he had been travelling from Lokitaung, on the same Sunday I would have been returning, in a beige four-wheel drive Hilux like mine when he noticed a vehicle following him. After ten kilometres he decided to drive off the road and park for a few minutes, since the other vehicle seemed reluctant to pass.

To his surprise the other vehicle did the same. The driver alighted carrying a pistol. He recognised him as Ekidor's driver. He asked him where he was going and more importantly still who he was carrying. John replied that he was alone. The would-be assailant checked all around lest someone was hiding and then climbed into his car and drove off without saying another word. Somebody somewhere was praying for my safety, or my Guardian Angel was doing overtime. Surviving that scare meant that I had to re-double my efforts to take safety precautions.

Peter Kiama, Damian Aryong and CJPC officials at the grave of Lomurudo Amo-doi, tortured to death in police cells in Turkana 1997

Maina Kiai in St. Augustine's Church, Lodwar, July 1997

2

A NEW DAWN IN TURKANA

The Catholic Justice and Peace Commission (CJPC) may have had humble and amateurish beginnings but it took root among the Turkana people in a way that neither the Church nor the government could have anticipated. This just confirms that the results of this work may have little to do with the efforts and toil of activists. It has everything to do with the seed that you are planting; it has a life of its own some produce thirty-fold, some sixty-fold and another one a hundred-fold, as the Gospel tells us.[3]

What one quickly realises in this work is that we do not possess or own the truth, justice or freedom. We are given it as a gift and it is ours to share with others. The seed of truth has a life of its own, we are just privileged to share it and to pass it on, water it and nurture it. The fruit of our planting is out of our hands and that is a very liberating fact. We should neither glorify our apparent successes nor be discouraged by what we think is failure. The seed may be germinating under the earth as we sleep and will produce the fruit at a time we least expect it to. This is best captured in what is frequently referred to as the Romero Prayer in honour of the slain Archbishop of San Salvador although it was written by Bishop Ken Untener of Saginaw[4]

> We plant the seeds that one day will grow,
>
> We water seeds already planted, knowing that they hold future promise.
>
> We lay foundations that will need further development
>
> We provide yeast that produces far beyond our capabilities,
>
> We cannot do everything and there is a sense of liberation in realising that.

---

3   Matthew 13:8

4   http://www.romerotrust.org.uk/romero-prayer

This enables us to do something, and do it very well[5].

It may be incomplete, but it is a beginning, a step along the way, an opportunity for the Lord's grace to enter and do the rest

We may never see the end results, but that is the difference between the master builder and the worker

We are workers not master builders; ministers, not messiahs

Prophets of a future not our own!

How true those words were in the life of the martyr, St Oscar Romero, as his death has inspired many people all around the world to take up the struggle for a more just world. He himself was quoted as saying that if he were killed his blood would continue to live on in the El Salvador people.

This was pretty much our thinking and inspiration as we expanded the work in Turkana. Our duty was to do what was right not to seek glory or fame, not to give up easily. It was enough to realise and accept that what we were doing was the work of God and that brought its own joy and fulfilment.

We soon discovered that networking was vital both for our development and security. While CJPC Lodwar was founded in 1994, it was the links we made with Kenya Human Rights Commission (KHRC) and its executive director, Maina Kiai, that gave us the confidence, support and standing in the community that we urgently needed. In March 1995 Maina came to stay with us for a week along with Ernest Murimi, the CJPC Coordinator for Nakuru Diocese in what we understood was an evaluation exercise.

What it turned out to be was an affirmation and team building exercise. We were on the right track; we just needed to put more shape on the organisation and the activities that we were involved in. Our presence was already felt on the ground as they both discovered when they travelled around. This partnership opened up new avenues and opportunities for us and added gravitas to our work and our standing

---

5

in society. We felt empowered and confident after that one week together.

The team were also exposed to national training through KHRC seminars and in the process made important linkages with other civil society organisations all over Kenya. At the same time CJPC was making major inroads in many other Catholic dioceses under the energetic leadership of Anthony Njui, the National Coordinator. Maina Kiai took a particular interest in our efforts, ever ready to give input, support and advice. It is often said that you meet the best people and form the strongest relationships in human rights work. My connection with Maina is a testimony to that as we are still very close friends after almost thirty years.

That support was most needed in 1995 and 1996 when we had to investigate the killings in police custody of two young Turkana herdsmen, one in Lockichar and the other 300 kilometres away in Lokichoggio. One was strangled to death with his own beads while the other was tortured until he could breathe no more. Those cases took years to get justice but the most immediate concern was to ensure that they acquired independent post-mortems and KHRC connected us with Dr Emily Rugene, then a young pathologist just back from studies in Europe. Emily still serves the country in the same capacity with a degree of humility, professionalism and integrity that is truly inspirational.

The extra-judicial killings of these young herdsmen brought a further spotlight on our work and the human rights violations going on in Turkana. In June 1997, I received a call from Maina with the news that Amnesty International Secretary General, Pierre Sana, was coming to the country and wished to visit our commission in Turkana. He was not coming alone as we found when two small planes landed on Lodwar Airstrip with a team of journalists and human rights defenders from the BBC, Independent Medico-Legal Unit (IMLU), KHRC, *Daily Nation* and several international media houses.

They were met on the airstrip by several Land Rovers of police, not there to welcome or protect them but to demand that they return to Nairobi. The instructions had come from the notorious District Commissioner, Reuben Rotich. However, the visitors were not deterred and we drove them from the airstrip to the County Headquarters to pay a courtesy visit to the same Mr Rotich. He left them waiting for some time and then only granted audience on condition that I would not be allowed to attend the meeting. Of course, this was not my first time to be ejected from the District Commissioner's Office. When I accompanied Bishop Mahon to protest at the harassment our team received from the security personnel several months previously, I was physically hauled out of his boardroom after being chased around his desk for a minute or two.

Anyhow, I did not need to be present to challenge Rotich on this occasion as both Maina Kiai and Ling Kituyi, Executive Director of the IMLU were very familiar with both the cases of extra-judicial killings and the constant harassment. A public meeting graced by our esteemed guests that was scheduled to be held in the Lokiriama Community Centre that evening had to be transferred to the Church when rowdy KANU youth wingers stoned the building. Nevertheless, hundreds bravely attended and listened to inspired sharing from Pierre Sana, Maina Kiai and Ling Kituyi.

Better still was that with the world's press in attendance the political terror from the ruling party and its cronies in the provincial administration was now exposed for all to see. Messrs Rotich and Ekidor might have been pleased with their show of might but ultimately their heavy handedness played into the hands of aspiring politicians and their supporters. This event might have marked the beginning of the end of the KANU dictatorship in Turkana County.

The Amnesty International visit occurred six months before the general election of 1997. For the first time since independence there emerged a host of young, educated, and qualified aspirants for the three parliamentary seats in the county. They could no longer be handpicked by KANU henchman nor rigged out by irregular counting of voters in broad daylight as I had witnessed in 1988. CJPC was particularly influential in the run up to the vote. It started by encouraging and monitoring the registration of voters. But its greatest impact was in the voter education that by now was reaching all ends of the vast county, which at close to 70,000 sq. km is about 80% of the size of the island of Ireland.

When it came to election time CJPC had a trained, accredited and commissioned poll monitor on every polling station in the whole of the county. This was no mean achievement as it took several months of recruitment, vetting and training not to mention the logistics in the deployment of every last one. I was assigned Lokitaung division, the hometown of the sitting MP, Japheth Ekidor as well as John Munyes, the Ford Kenya opposition candidate, who had been my student at Lodwar High School in 1983. For our safety we kept secret our constituencies of supervision. However, this constituency of Turkana North was considered to be the one that would be the most volatile and most competitive.

Turkana voters giving the opposition Ford Kenya salute in December 1997 polls

On voting day, I travelled from station to station checking on the monitors. However, I had to intervene at one stage and demand that the police and the returning officer stop Ekidor's wife from interfering with the process at several polling stations. They duly cooperated and the voting ended peacefully or so we thought. However, the National Electoral Commission extended the voting by one day. So late in the evening I had to revisit all the monitors and request them to not depart from their stations as the voting materials could be tampered with. Another day's voting or idling, call it what you will, before the counting would begin.

The monitors then had to accompany the tally sheets and the ballot boxes on the four-hour journey to Kakuma where the final tallying was to be completed. That took another day before John Munyes was announced as the duly elected MP for Turkana North on a Ford Kenya ticket, the first non KANU representative since independence. Now at last, for the first time, it was okay to be in the opposition and for the people the victory was as much due to the efforts of CJPC as Munyes' team. Had it not been for continuous and extensive civic education as well as poll monitors, this election would have been rigged at many stages of the process just as had happened on previous occasions and the public would have been denied the chance to elect a representative of their choice.

As I drove out of Turkana in early January 1998 and said goodbye to my home for fifteen years, I had the satisfaction of knowing that change had taken place and in some small or big way, we at CJPC had facilitated it. We had witnessed the people of Turkana demand that their votes should count, that their voices be heard and that their leaders be held accountable. This was the time democracy in all its purest and broadest sense arrived in the desert.

We had planted the seeds without realising that they could produce fruit and change in ways that we could not have possibly imagined. We were indeed prophets of 'a future not our own'. There was also the comfort of knowing that I was handing over the reins to a most worthy successor, Peter Kiama. He spent four more years in Turkana before moving on to Kenya Human Rights Commission, Trócaire and currently at Independent Medico-Legal Unit (IMLU) where he continues as Executive Director to defend victims of torture, brutality and extra-judicial killing, carrying on from where he started in Turkana.

I was then granted a short sabbatical by my Society and returned to take up the role of CJPC Coordinator for Kitale Diocese in October 1998. Kitale had just been made a new diocese after being carved out of from Eldoret and Maurice Crowley, a fellow St Patrick's Missionary priest had been appointed as the first bishop. It was a new adventure for him and for me as I came to grasp the challenges of two very different counties, West Pokot and Trans Nzoia. Yet I felt ready for that challenge.

3

HUNTED IN WEST POKOT
BY FRANCIS POLISI LOTODO

✣

A quarter of a century ago, West Pokot was like no other county in the Republic of Kenya. While the constitution may have been amended in 1992 to allow more than one political party to promote its policies and candidates, West Pokot remained a closed zone. In many ways it resembled the colonial closed districts as we recall that the place name Keringet, on the borders with Trans Nzoia, was derived from the 'green gate' that the settlers put on the Kapenguria to Lodwar road to prevent outsiders from accessing the Northern Frontier Districts. Trans Nzoia was alive and the home of opposition politics while Pokot still waved the one finger salute of KANU.

Not much had changed since independence with Francis Polisi Lotodo anointed and feared as the supreme and all-powerful authoritarian figure in the county. Lotodo was a bit of an enigma; extremely loyal to KANU and Daniel arap Moi yet occasionally overstepping his perceived powers with Moi arraigning him in court on frivolous charges in both the 70s and 80s. Yet, Moi depended on him greatly and it was Lotodo he turned to in August 1982 during the attempted coup when his security was at risk and the only safe place was provided in Turkwell Gorge on the Pokot-Turkana border.

Pokot had eighty county councillors handpicked by Lotodo, mostly illiterate, belligerent and extremely submissive. Despite its commitment to the KANU ideology the county remained among the poorest, most marginalised and deprived in the nation. The only electricity outside Kapenguria town was the eight kilometres of national grid that extended to Lotodo's Parua home. Were it not for the Catholic Church and a few donor organisations there would be few if any children reaching secondary school. Lotodo of course didn't worry. What bothered him was not the illiterate population but the educated, those who could think and talk for themselves and ask questions about their needs and development.

So, while it was a pretty easy task to establish the Catholic Justice and Peace Commission (CJPC) in Kitale, it was quite another matter altogether to establish a presence in Kapenguria, 40 kilometres away. However, what gave me the courage and the impetus was a chance meeting with a young man from Lelan Division, who had just finished a Bachelor of Education Degree in Moi University, Eldoret. David Pkosing was quite bold and full of confidence when he came inquiring about a job. When I asked if he was ready to take on the responsibility of starting an office and giving us a visible, assertive and permanent presence in West Pokot, he replied in the affirmative.

It took a few months for him to familiarise himself with the challenges ahead and to find a suitable and safe environment but he received very good mentorship from the Trans Nzoia coordinator, Davis Wafula. Eventually, through the kindness of Kenya National Union of Teachers (KNUT) we were offered space for an office at their headquarters in Kapenguria. It was a very humble beginning but it made a huge impact, as much because of the curiosity that it provoked as due to its own achievements. Initially, we dealt with the immediate concerns of the local population namely police harassment, misuse of famine relief food and child neglect.

When we then started doing basic civic and voter education, however, the word reached Mr Lotodo's ears through his many sycophants and informers. By then the content had gained legs and the ever-paranoid Minister denounced our work in public claiming that we were planning to overthrow the government with arms supplied by the Irish Republican Army (IRA). A training of Civic Educators in Active Non-Violence by Chemchemi ya Ukweli was violently disrupted in Tartar Pastoral Centre by Lotodo's goons and several other meetings had to be cancelled at the last moment due to threats of interference from other idlers.

Of course, when he called for my deportation along with that of Bishop Crowley, the public became all the more curious and interested in our work. More and more parishes and groups began to request us to come and enlighten them on the proposed constitutional reform process as well as providing a forum for discussion on more local issues. A quiet revolution was taking place and Lotodo could not show any restraint or prudence in addressing it.

As a means of advancing our work, we planned at the end of January 1999 a procession and a Mass in Kapenguria led by Bishop Crowley in support of the inclusion of the faith based Ufungamano Initiative in the Constitutional Process. The Bishop encouraged as many priests and Christians to attend as possible. However, Lotodo could not allow this to take place in his own backyard. He arranged with the local OCPD to seal off the church and prevent us from processing through the

29

Priest threatened with death

**By JOSEPH OLWENY
and GEORGE OMONSO**

A Catholic priest yesterday received death threats in a letter mailed to him.

Father Gabriel Dolan of the Kitale Peace and Justice Commission said the letter, written in Kiswahili, demands that he leaves Trans-Nzoia District or else he will be killed.

The priest, who has been involved in civic education in the North Rift, said he was trailed by unknown people for three days before he received the threats.

The letter reads in part: "*Tunasikitika sana kwamba wewe unahusika kwa kupeana vyakula, pesa, mabunduki na marisasi ili Wakenya waweze kufanya vita vya wenyewe kwa wenyewe. Chagua*

Kitale Catholic clergyman accused of supplying guns, ammo

ufe ama uishi kwa amani na Wakenya ama utakumbuka Kenya siku zote ukiwa kaburini." (We are sad that you are involved in giving relief food, money, guns and ammunition so that Kenyans can fight one another. Choose death or a peaceful life with Kenyans; otherwise you will remember Kenya in your grave).

Yesterday, a shaken Fr Dolan reported the matter to the Kitale police station. Local police boss Alfred Ng'etich said investigations into the

matter have started.

The developments come barely a week after Cherangany MP Kipruto Kirwa said that threats to kill Fr Dolan and evict another priest in Keiyo. Fr Michael Rop, should not be taken lightly.

Mr Kirwa demanded the arrest of a nominated councillor, Mr Pius Kauka, who had threatened to lead Sabaot youth in killing Fr Dolan over a disputed 2,000-acre farm.

Father Dolan has been fighting for the

settlement of squatters and victims of tribal clashes on land formerly known as John Smith Farm. The farm is now owned by Mokwo Co-operative Society.

Over the weekend, Assistant Minister Samuel Moroto said he and Fr Dolan had resolved their differences. Mr Moroto, who is also the Kapenguria MP, had previously declared war on the priest, accusing him of inciting the public and being against the interests of the Pokot.

Meanwhile, two church leaders in West Pokot have welcomed Mr Moroto's decision to work with Fr Dolan.

The Rev John Lodinyo of the Baptist Church and the Rev Julius Murgor of the African Inland Church said the development would bring peace in the district.

town. By then the church was full and two dozen priests were robed. As police in riot gear and equipped with tear gas canisters sealed the church gates, we decided this was not the opportune moment for Bishop Crowley to have his first taste of tear gas. Instead, we chose to just process along the perimeter hedge of the church and then proceed with the Mass indoors.

However, Lotodo considered this defiance, and carried out a series of meetings calling for my deportation which of course raised our profile and brought more attention to the work we were doing.[6] In one of those unlicensed demonstrations his followers burnt an effigy of me in Kapenguria. He was running scared without any legitimate reason but by then we were getting courageous and becoming established. The Kenya Human Rights Commission (KHRC) and the daily newspapers condemned his utterances and called for our protection and security.[7] This was no longer a local, village matter but it gave our humble efforts a high profile and ironically provided us with more security[8]

Lotodo, however, did not confine himself to threats in public meetings, he also brought his concerns and demands to Mr Moi in State House. In early 2000, the members of parliament for Pokot and Turkana communities were called to State House to discuss the deteriorating security situation along the common border in which several dozen had been killed in recent cattle rustling incidents. Lotodo was no friend of the Turkana community nor of their elected representatives.

Within a month of that State House meeting, the three Turkana MPs all contacted me and informed me about what was requested by Lotodo and how Daniel arap Moi responded. David Ethuro, Francis Ewoton and John Munyes had been close associates of mine for some years in Turkana so they felt obliged to disclose the contents of the private meeting. Briefly, Lotodo had asked the President to expel me but he rather curtly replied in an obscure manner that why could such a powerful figure like Lotodo not deal with a simple foreigner himself without dragging him into the conflict. Did it indicate that Lotodo and KANU were losing their grip on the County?

The three legislators expressed concern that the remarks indicated that Moi was

---

6   https://www.nation.co.ke/news/1056-374262-l7x8obz/index.html

7   People Daily, August 17th 1999

8   People Daily, February 4th 2000; Daily Nation Editorial, February 3rd 2000; Sunday View; Gitau Wargi February 6th 2000, Sunday Nation

Fair, Frank and Fearless Tel: 794636 Nairobi

Daily

ISSUE NO. 694   Monday, October 30, 2000   PRICE: Shs 30/-

Clashes: Catholics want Moi apology

Govt demands Shs 200 million from Swipco

By MATHEWS NDANYI

THE government is now demanding a refund of close to Shs 200 million paid out by the Treasury to the controversial Inspection and Control Services (ICS) Limited better known as Swipco.

The firm was hired to audit pre-shipment inspection firms (PSIs) and the customs department operations in international trade.

The permanent secretary in the ministry of finance Martin Luke Oduor-Otieno has officially written to the firm, expressing dissatisfaction at its operations in Kenya. He has notified the ICS managing director David K. Andere that the firm was excessively paid by the Treasury for services not rendered.

The letter, signed by E. M. Githae for the PS, says that since the contract was awarded to ICS on April 3, 1998, the firm had invoiced the treasury for payments of more than Shs 116 million (US $ 1,425,000). He said most of the money has already been paid out to the firm whose operations have elicited an outcry.

THE chairman of the commission to review land laws, Charles Mugane Njonjo, was stunned over the weekend when the Catholic church asked him to petition President Moi to apologise on behalf of the government for its active role in the land clashes.

By LEONARD WEKESA

This, the priest said, would be a huge gesture towards reconciliation and national unity.

The Kitale Catholic Justice and Peace Commission director, Father Gabriel Dolan, stunned the commission further when he challenged the head of state to facilitate the prosecution of key instigators and organisers of the tribal clashes that rocked the country in the run up to the reintroduction of the second multiparty epoch in Kenya's politics.

Addressing the cheering crowd at the Kitale museum hall, the priest demanded that the findings of the Akiwumi commission on tribal clashes be made public to erase fears that

the government participated in the genocide and assure Kenyans that it was committed to reconcile with the victims of the clashes.

The priest said that the issue of ethnic clashes will haunt the government so long as it remained in power, adding that the victims had lost confidence and trust in government and its machinery.

"Despite the report on the Kiliku inquiry and the public evidence given to the Akiwumi commission, the Kanu government still denies any responsibility for the clashes yet that is in fact the case ... why has the government not released the report of the commission?" Dolan

Turn to Page 2

Church calls for probe on threat to kill priest

By NATION Correspondents

Church leaders in the North Rift have called for investigations into death threats against a Kitale Catholic priest.

Led by Anglican Rev Maritim Rirei and church official Leonard Ndiema, the clerics described the threats against Fr Gabriel Dolan as "serious" and told the police to act swiftly.

On Wednesday, Fr Dolan, the Kitale Catholic Justice and Peace Commission director, received an anonymous letter telling him to leave Trans Nzoia District or be killed.

Fr Dolan has been vocal in agitating for the rights of squatters, the fight against torture and civic education.

A frequent critic of the government, Fr Dolan has also called for the disarming of some communities in the North Rift to end cattle-rustling and banditry.

The church leaders said priests have in the past received such threats but police delayed investigations until "the men of God died in mysterious circumstances".

The leaders said the government should guarantee all Kenyans their right to life and crack down on those threatening to kill others. Fr Dolan, who has recorded statements with the police, claimed that unknown people trailed him for three days before he received the death threats.

allowing Lotodo to deal with me as he deemed fit. My response was to dismiss it all lightly while appreciating their concern for my welfare. Anyhow, within a few months' things were to change drastically in the area with the sudden passing of Lotodo in November 2000.

In October, the Minister had sent an emissary to Bishop Crowley and I seeking reconciliation and an improvement in relations. It was all rather bizarre as the Kapenguria Mayor was humble and amicable. He asked me for a message to bring back to Lotodo. I bluntly replied that I was aware that Moi was one of the chief suspects in the death of Fr Kaiser in August of the same year, but that if they had similar plans for me, they should think again because I would come back from the afterlife to haunt Lotodo and make his life miserable. There was no malintent on my behalf but I was aware that he was a superstitious man who regularly visited witchdoctors, so it was good to use that knowledge for my own protection.

However, when in a few weeks Lotodo was called away from this life, I felt a certain trepidation and regret. Had the message been delivered to him before his passing or was it shared with his family and close supporters? I left it all in the hands of God and went to the airstrip at Kapenguria to receive the body and to condole with the family. I left the funeral Mass and burial in the capable hands of Bishop Crowley.

The passing of Lotodo marked a massive change in the politics of the District with new faces elected by a popular vote. One of those was David Pkosing who after two unsuccessful attempts in 2002 and 2007 elections was finally chosen as the Pokot North MP in 2013. He was re-elected in the 2017 general election. But the legend of Lotodo is embedded in the Pokot memory and in generations to come he will continue to be remembered if not revered. Interestingly, his son Augustine Monges – a different personality altogether - is currently employed as CEC Lands in the County Government and we continue to interact on matters of mutual interest.

4

SQUATTERS IN A LAND OF PLENTY

✠

Trans Nzoia is probably the most beautiful and most fertile county in the Republic of Kenya. With a reliable rainfall pattern, moderate temperatures and a mean altitude of 1,800 metres it makes life relatively easy and provides a delightful environment for its inhabitants. The colonial settlers quickly identified this as a special area among the White Highlands in the Rift Valley. They established a thriving agricultural economy including maize, fruit, horticulture and dairy farming.

When independence came, most settlers chose to leave although a few families have stayed up until today. Through its land settlement programme, the Ministry of Lands developed and implemented settlement schemes to include the former colonial farm labourers and the many squatters in the county. The settlers also handed over Agricultural Development Corporation (ADC) Farms, research estates like Kenya Agriculture Research Institute (KARI), large tracts of land at Kitale Farm Prison, and many other public institutions to the new independent government.

However, the tribesmen and the cronies of successive independence regimes also recognised the opportunity to be settled as 'landless' in the land of plenty. The whole settlement scheme programme was established to settle the landless and to make these settlement schemes an integrated programme that would help to bring unity and harmony among the diverse ethnic groups in the country. For that reason, each scheme should have had a 60:40 ratio in the allocation, 60% local people and 40% from outside the area. This rarely if ever happened.

What in fact happened in Trans Nzoia was that cronies of Jomo Kenyatta and Daniel arap Moi frequently brought their own tribesmen and allocated them land in a single settlement scheme. So, you may find several schemes that were entirely allocated to one ethnic community. They may have come from afar but ended up naming the adopted areas according to their native villages where they came from. Instead of having mixed ethnic communities you find settlement schemes for Kisii, Kikuyu, Nandi, Teso, Meru etc and they lived together pretty much as they did before in their former home districts. Integration rarely if ever took place although today the younger generation are more inclined to marry outside their own ethnic community.

34

However, in this skewed allocation programme the local Bukusu and Sabaot communities frequently were omitted in the allocation exercise and were reduced to being mere squatters in their own homeland. This produced a lot of resentment against outsiders and brought endemic poverty to the locals. Besides, while most schemes were granting allotees either two and a half or five acres of land, there were often huge portions of twenty acres and above set aside in each scheme to politicians who used their own tribesmen as cover, security and farm labourers.

When the settlement scheme programme was drawing to a close the land grabbers now turned their attention to every other piece of available government land in the area. So, some Agricultural Development Corporation (ADC) and Kenyan Agricultural and Research Institute (KARI) farms were shared out among the nation's looters. Even prison land was not safe, nor parks or forests.

Moi dished out huge tracts all over the country delegating authority to the Commissioner of Lands to allocate on his behalf. According to the Ndungu Commission of Inquiry there were up to 200,000 illegally or irregularly allocated land titles in the country probably amounting to between three and four million acres of land in the wrong hands. A considerable portion of this grabbed land was in Trans Nzoia. In research conducted by CJPC we discovered that there were roughly 72,000 acres of illegally allocated land in the county of Trans Nzoia alone.[9]

Of course, referring to this as such was just the polite, legal definition; the truth was that it was stolen from the poor and deserving by the ruling class. Kenya Land Alliance together with the Kenya National Commission on Human Rights (KNCHR) in research published as Unjust Enrichment estimated that a few dozen politicians benefited to the tune of Kshs 53bn through land they stole from the public reserve.[10]The great inequality and injustice in the land sector was visible everywhere. The squatters, or those living on plots of fifty by one hundred feet, were the majority, eking out a living for their families.

To address injustice and poverty then meant that we had to attend to the issue of land no matter how contentious or dangerous that work might be. To address the land problem was in turn to confront the political establishment and the corrupt systems that permitted such fraud and theft of public land. Put another way, land was

---

9   Gabriel Dolan, LLM Dissertation, UUJ, 'No Transition Without Addressing the Land Question', September 2007

10   http://www.kenyalandalliance.or.ke/download/unjust-enrichment-volume-2-the-mak ing-of-land-grabbing-millionaires/?wpdmdl=2674&refresh=5ea187a7123581587644327

not just an economic problem it was also a political one and we could not expect to get much sympathy or cooperation from those in authority at any level since for the most part they were either current beneficiaries, or aspired to benefit from their period of employment in the area with one or two titles for their own families.

Land activists in Kenya, therefore, face horrific hurdles in their work. They may have the poor and the dispossessed among their supporters but the odds are strongly stacked against them. However, the professional and moral support that we received from the Kenya Land Alliance (KLA) gave us enormous encouragement and provided many strategies on how to build a movement around the issue of land. The KLA Coordinator was Odenda Lumumba, a seasoned human rights defender and a former political prisoner under Moi. He had received a good foundation in advocacy with Maina Kiai and other activists at the Kenya Human Rights Commission (KHRC) and he coordinated KLA with courage, brilliance and considerable success for a quarter of a century.

Mindful from the outset that the landless must become organised, be disciplined and focused, we spent a lot of time moulding the leadership of two groups. One was the Trans Nzoia Squatters Alliance and the other the Internally Displaced People (IDPs) who had been dispossessed during the clashes of 1992 and 1997. Both these groups eventually discovered that they had a voice because they had the numbers and a just cause. What they merely required was organisation, support, and a forum to vent their anger and hopes.

Liberation theology speaks at length about the option for the poor, taking the side of the dispossessed and viewing life from the perspective of the poorest and most forgotten. Pope Francis speaks of them with fondness and honesty when he says, 'The excluded are not the "exploited" but the outcast, the "leftovers"'.[11] Others often refer to them as the least and the last.

What is frequently forgotten is that the poor are the majority, they have a voice and they can change the world if the rest of us would dare to listen to them. The wisdom, humility, hope and friendships acquired from interacting with these two groups are something that will remain with me for a very long time indeed. We should not dare to speak on their behalf but give them space and a forum where they can speak for themselves.

---

11   Evangelii Gaudium, No 53

Another lesson learned from my time in Kitale is that those who suffer the most must be willing to invest in their own liberation. What that meant in practice is that we never paid transport or lunch allowance for public demonstrations and we sold T-shirts to them at a discounted price. The struggle is theirs and they must invest their energy, time and few shillings if it is at all to succeed. Protests in Kitale on the land issue frequently attracted several thousand marchers all of whom found their own way by matatu, bicycle or foot to the venue. They returned by the same means and were only provided with drinking water to quench their thirst in the midday sun.

However, the experience of human rights work in Mombasa was a wholly different experience. I was horrified to discover that protesters were frequently paid and that T-Shirts were given out freely even when folk could not understand the message they contained. Human rights work had been commercialised on the coast and in many parts of Kenya. Crowds are for hire, just as for political rallies and for that reason the impact has been limited despite the growing number of organisations springing up along the way.

That is not to deny that there are some extraordinarily committed and brave human rights defenders everywhere. However, for many, human rights work is a career choice and frequently civil society organizations (CSOs) can become obstacles in the realisation of justice, when they create dependency and operate through gatekeepers, rather than empowering the communities that they claim they are serving. Human rights people must know it is not about themselves but it is the people who really matter. That means in effect that this work must concentrate on building human rights communities over long periods of time, pretty much in the same manner that the Church carries out its own mission. It is about relationships, organisation, structures and empowerment and that requires time, commitment, self-sacrifice and patience.

The landless and dispossessed in Kitale were aware that for them to be allocated land they must prevent further grabbing of public land and equally demand that illegally acquired land be repossessed and distributed among the more deserving and needy. In June 2001 the government announced the sale of the 3,018-acre ADC farm, called Old Ngatongo. We objected to this sale on the grounds that the buyer would almost certainly be a well-connected tycoon who would acquire it at a throwaway price to the detriment of the many landless who could have ac-quired it through a cooperative purchase.[12] The auction was cancelled after our

---

12   Daily Nation, June 21st 2001

intervention although there were no plans put in place to distribute it among the poor.[13] Still, it demonstrated that complaints could and should be addressed and that, if enough noise was made, someone somewhere might listen or have their consciences pricked.

The two aggrieved communities were very familiar with happenings in their areas and soon brought to our attention the irregular allocation of the 1,500 acres that was part of Kitale Phase III scheme, land that had once been ADC property. The most obvious beneficiaries of the land should have been those who were evicted from Kiborora Forest in 1987 but senior government officials had been targeting the land for themselves and the list of beneficiaries included MPs from Turkana, Pokot and Trans Nzoia.

That allocation was cancelled by President Moi and the repeat allocation was more favourable to the deserving. However, a mistake in the allocation was to once again favour one ethnic group rather than several. As a result, clashes have frequently erupted in the scheme between those who missed out and those who acquired the land.

Similar problems have arisen on the Kanyarakwet land on the borders of Pokot and Trans Nzoia. There has been no revocation of the list of beneficiaries to date despite the fact that current MPs in Pokot are farming the land while the poor on either side of the border squabble over the remnants. Politicians may appear to defend their own people in these conflicts but in fact they are defending the land that they acquired on behalf of their own landless people. A further travesty of justice.

Of course, the campaign to repossess public land was not just about defending the poor. It also aspired to instil a sense of patriotism and pride in the general public with regard to the protection of shared public spaces. In that respect we focused on the issues of Kitale Farm Prison and Kitale Park. The prison was overcrowded with up to 4,000 prisoners, yet prison commissioners and commanders, as well as chiefs and politicians, had taken over 3,000 acres for their own possession. The park was the only green space left in Kitale town where the public could relax and feel secure. It too was under threat.

The Commissioner of Prisons, Abraham Kamakil, had taken up to two hundred acres of the Prison Farm for himself and begun construction of a palatial house.

---

13   https://www.nation.co.ke/news/1056-337414-lac9uiz/index.html

This edifice soon became the focus of our attention as it identified the head of prisons and his involvement in grabbing of public land. Through media reports and letters to the Minister for Home Affairs, Mr Moody Awori, we demanded an intervention in 2003 if the newly elected government of Mwai Kibaki was serious about its claim to be fighting corruption.

To provoke and encourage the government into more corrective engagement on the land issue, we arranged the first major demonstration in Kitale on May 19th 2003. The event was flagged off by Vice President Kijana Wamalwa in what proved to be his last official function in Kenya. He thereafter flew off to Switzerland to attend the International Labour Organisation conference. There he took ill and was transferred to London for treatment where he remained until his demise in August of that year.

But the hundreds of protestors were empowered and delighted with Wamalwa's support and solidarity and they proceeded to march around the town pointing out the land and institutions that had been illegally acquired. These properties included Mount Elgon Hospital as well as several schools and a forest that had been excised and a filling station and supermarket constructed on the land. The protestors found riot police at the entrance to most of the contested properties but that did not deter them from erecting their signboards that read, 'This land is public property, give it back now'.[14] The Swahili version of the same slogan read, Ardhi ya Umma Uradhi Wetu, Rudisha Sasa.

The hospital together with the land of the fuel station had illegally fallen into the hands of Nathanial Tum, the Executive Director of Kenya Seed Company, a state corporation. Tum was Moi's right-hand man in the area and he later endeavoured to privatise Kenya Seed into his own hands a few years later by selling the majority of shares to himself. The courts, fortunately, found this arrangement illegal while the hospital was eventually restored as a public entity.

The support of the Vice President and the presence of such a vast crowd gave energy, standing and credibility to the lands campaign. More came aboard to support while others who had documentation on grabbed land in the area brought it to our offices for consideration. As the dynamism increased and the campaign gained popularity, we launched a petition to the Ministry of Lands to repossess all grabbed land in the republic. The petition got 28,000 signatures in a month and we were

---

14   Standard, May 20th 2003

invited by Lands Minister Amos Kimunya to Nairobi to hand over the petition. He seized the opportunity to call the media houses to his office and to reiterate that he was grateful for our initiative and to state that the National Rainbow Coalition (NARC) government would take serious action on the same.

Within a matter of weeks, the Lands Ministry established a Commission of Inquiry[15] into all illegally allocated land in the Republic. The Commission was popularly known as the Ndungu Commission[16] after its Chair Paul Ndungu and its membership offered considerable hope that the government was committed to thorough investigation and to implementation of the Commission's recommendations.

The Catholic Justice and Peace Commission (CJPC) was very enthusiastic about this initiative and began compiling all its research for submission. We were given a special hearing by the Commission and handed over half a dozen box files of documentation on grabbed land in Trans Nzoia. When the report was finally released our efforts were noted and acknowledged.[17]

The commission travelled the country and produced a very thorough report that was clear in its analysis, findings and recommendations. But there was a huge delay in releasing the report and this caused us to organise another protest in November 2004 demanding its release. In attendance was Maina Kiai, Koigi Wamwere, Khelef Khalifa and Odenda Lumumba who himself had been on the Commission of Inquiry Team. Responding to the protests, Lands Minister Kimunya released the report the following week. The question, however, was would it ever be implemented? Would it gather dust in government offices or would we need to exert even pressure to have the report implemented and funded? That challenge we took up with vigour.

---

15   June 30th Special Gazette Notice
16   https://en.wikipedia.org/wiki/Ndungu_Land_Commission
17   Page31, Ndungu Commission of Inquiry

Presenting Lands Minister Amos Kimunya with T Shirt that translates as 'Public Land is Our Heritage' 2003;

Land: Priest chides Kanu, Narc regimes

By MONICA MUTHWII

SENIOR politicians and civil servants in the present and former government have been implicated in land grabbing in Trans Nzoia district.

The justice and peace committee of the Catholic Diocese of Kitale told the lands and settlement minister Amos Kimunya that over 85 percent of the 3, 400 acres of the Kitale Prison Farm were dished out to senior prison officials in 1999.

The committee led by Father Gabriel Dolan also told the minister that the Kenya Agricultural Research Institute (KARI) and KEPHIS farms in the district have been decimated and their staff houses forcibly taken.

The committee, which paid the minister a courtesy call at his Ardhi House office, said primary schools such as St Joseph's, Trans Nzoia and Kitale Academy have also lost their land to grabbers.

The members of the committee said other public institutions that have been grabbed include Mt Elgon hospital, the first public medical facility in the area, which has been privatised, land from Kitale District Hospital, ADC farms and road and railway reserves.

The group presented the minister with 28,000 signatures from the locals who have petitioned the government to move in fast and reclaim the land and property.

Public Forum on land in Kitale, February 2004 – L to R – The late Opiato Odindo. Odenda Lumumba, Kenya Land Alliance, Maina Kiai, Chair KNCHR, Commissioner Khelef Khalifa, KNCHR.

Peaceful demonstrations in Kitale on land matters in 2005

Presenting Mr. Kimunya with Poster with demand to repossess stolen land;

he minister for lands and human settlements Amos Kimunya looks at a petition brought to im by Father Gabriel Dolan, the director Catholic Justce Peace and Commission Kitale, after resenting complaints of land grabbing to the minister at his Ardhi House office yesterday LILIAN NYAMBURA

42

FROM PRISON LAND TO PRISON CELLS

The grabbing of Kitale Farm Prison Land became a regular news item in the country thanks to the commitment of a few journalists of integrity. Waithaka Waihenya of the East African Standard devoted a whole page to the issue in October 2003, including a photograph of the two-storey house being constructed by the Prison Commissioner but now abandoned after our earlier revelations.[18]

Seven days later the same newspaper published, under their Right of Reply section, two responses, one from the Vice President's Press Service[19] and the other from the Public Relations Office of the Commissioner of Prisons. The Prisons Department denied that the construction was illegal while Awori committed himself to visit the venue himself on 6 November.[20] This seemed like significant progress following our efforts to investigate and expose the matter.

Several Catholic Justice and Peace Commission activists from the neighbouring parish of St Josephs suggested that we should not miss the opportunity to witness the Vice President's visit and if at all possible, to meet him. They went ahead to compose a poem about the land that they would recite to Mr Awori when he alighted from his vehicle to view the disputed house. We were a small group of half a dozen and we made sure to stay off the main road and also to park our vehicle off road.

However, a few minutes before the entourage appeared the Kitale Police arrived and arrested four of us, crudely manhandling us and dumping us on to their Land Rover. The others were Boniface Wanyoike, Patrick Wafula and Thomas Kariuki.

Fortunately, the whole incident was captured by the cameras of two TV stations. The arrest was the first item on the evening news of both NTV and KTN on 6 November. The following day's newspapers carried detailed reports of the incident as well as photographs of my arrest. There was quite an uproar but we were not to

---

18   Kitale's long wait for Moody Awori, East African Standard, October 22nd 2003.

19   Moody Awori replaced the late Kijana Wamalwa as Vice President in August 2003.

20   East African Standard, October 30th 2003

know as we spent five hours in the Kitale Police cells after the Officer Commanding Police Station (OCS) Isaac Kasembeli had punched, kicked and beaten me as I alighted from the police Land Rover and on my way to the police cells.

When it passed 6pm in the evening we were pretty sure of spending the night in the cells as police regulations forbid release under any circumstances after that hour. However, at around 7.30pm the cell doors were unlocked and the officers on duty rather unenthusiastically ordered us to collect our personal items and get out. There was no mention of a bond or cash bail and we didn't inquire either.

Awori is reported to have ordered our release but more notably still he never commented about the status of Kitale Farm Prison land after his visit there. That was more telling. But the incident did not end there as on the following day, human rights defenders protested in Nairobi and called for Awori to speak out on the matter of the land. There were also many calls for the OCS to be interdicted.

We went back to the police station the following day to record statements but in the light of the outrage the officers were more civil and cautious in their dealings with us. My complaint about the beating was recorded in the Occurrence Book (OB) and I filled the mandatory P3 Report Form but no investigation ever took place despite my many return visits to check on developments. However, it took four more days for our vehicle to be released as the police demanded towing charges which we refused to pay as the car was not in any way causing an obstruction from where it was removed.

What happened that day shocked many Kenyans not because of the excess of the police mistreatment but the fact that this NARC government was not behaving any differently toward dissent and protests than that of the Moi regime.[21] This was a test case and they had failed miserably. Put another way, incidents like this marked the end of the honeymoon period of the new Kibaki government in the public's eyes. It was clearly business as usual.

The matter remained in the news for quite some time, however. The Anglican Church in Eldoret was quick to express support yet Archbishop Raphael Ndingi of Nairobi was critical of my behaviour. While saying that the police should not have used excessive force, he nevertheless warned that I should have forwarded my memorandum to Awori through my own Bishop in Kitale. He went on to say, 'Fr

---

21   Saturday Nation, Editorial November 8th 2003

Dolan should have anticipated the police reaction as the matter was serious'.[22]

However, the Chairman of the Kenya Bishops Conference, Bishop Cornelius Korir of Eldoret, had a different view and speaking on behalf of all the Bishops in the country, he said, 'Fr Dolan had every right to meet the Vice President and the police treatment of him was unjustifiable and unacceptable'.[23] That expression of support was critical as the remarks by Ndingi had left all of us very vulnerable to attacks of any nature from any quarters. The incident did not go unnoticed by the international press as evidenced by this excerpt from the Irish Times.[24]

What was most encouraging also was that the priests and faithful of Kitale Diocese organised a demonstration of support. Besides, a letter of support from the Papal Nuncio in Kenya, Archbishop Giovanni Tonucci was a further indication that we had not committed any offence and that the Pope's representative was 'in solidarity with our efforts to live the gospel of justice and peace'.

A week later, OCS Kasembeli as well as the Officer Commanding Police Division and CID were all transferred out of Kitale. It did appear that this was a disciplinary move. However, it was all short-lived as Kasembeli was later deployed as a trainer at Police Training headquarters in Kaiganjo. He obviously was now encouraged to induct the new police recruits into his crude methods of handling peaceful protests.

The Prisons department claimed that they would repossess all of their grabbed land.[25] The Ndungu Commission of inquiry did visit the Kitale Farm as well as ADC Farms in December and confirmed the list of the beneficiaries.[26] There was no reference to Kamakil in that list but 'grabbers' usually listed family members as beneficiaries rather than themselves. Yet, if the construction of the house was regular and legal as claimed by the Prisons department, then why did the work stop when we first asked questions? Even today the derelict building remains as a monument to our efforts at exposing the corruption in the Home Affairs Ministry. The prison continued to claim back segments of its own land but mostly that responsibility was left to the officer in charge of Kitale Prison rather than with the outright support from headquarters or the lands ministry.

22 Daily Nation, November 11th 2003

23 Daily Nation, November 12th 2003

24 https://www.irishtimes.com/news/irish-priest-alleges-assault-after-arrest-in-kenya
    1.390360

25 Daily Nation, November 18th 2003

26 https://www.nation.co.ke/news/1056-272742-lr296vz/index.html

Another piece of public land already mentioned that was of particular concern to the community was that of Kitale Public Park. Together with the Green Belt Movement of Wangari Maathai we began lobbying about its security as early as 1999. A businessman claimed to have a title deed for the disputed public space and he proceeded to sue both CJPC and the Green Belt movement to prevent us from interfering with his property. The case was heard in December 2000 and we were represented by the late Kwanza MP, George Kapten, in what proved to be his last public interest litigation case before his sudden demise on Christmas Day the same year.

Before the ruling was given by Kitale High Court Judge, Alnashir Visram,[27] Mr Kapten scribbled a quick note and discreetly put it in my hand. It read, 'we are going to lose this case, so if you are going to do something on the site, you better do it immediately'. We left the court promptly and a group of twenty activists headed for the disputed land. The group of protestors included Wafula Buke and Odenda Lumumba of Kenya Human Rights Commission. Within ten minutes we had destroyed the recently constructed wall and perimeter fence on the town's only public park. The developer left the court elated. However, the smile was quickly removed from his face with the sight of dust and smoke emerging from his walled premises. We had sent a message that there are many ways to find justice in Kenya. The struggle was not to end there.

To mark World Environmental Day in 2003, we planted trees in the Park and raised a billboard to rename the park, George Kapten Memorial Park. The ceremony was performed by the late legislator's widow and family. The park took on a new significance through that naming ceremony. In Kitale, the park once more became the centre of attention in 2005 as the so-called 'private developer' began to construct another perimeter wall. The community became so enraged that they demanded that we resist. After contacting Lands Minister Amos Kimunya, we gave him two weeks to repossess the land or else the community would assist him in doing the honourable thing in protecting it for use by the public.

No reply was forthcoming and so we planned a protest event for early August 2005. The District Security Committee pleaded with us to abandon the protests. However, this time the community would not stand down. A crowd of five hundred marched to the site and promptly started the demolition. Police initially stood at a

---

27   High Court of Kenya, Eldoret: Civil Case No 207 of 1999

distance but eventually the riot squad stormed the park with rubber bullets and tear gas, while shooting live bullets in the air.

Twenty-two people were arrested, and these were mainly older protestors and women with infant children. The police searched desperately for me but thanks to the quickness of mind of a maid in a nearby hotel I found safety in a single toilet which she duly locked from the outside. The police searched every room in the building but never uncovered my hiding place. In the dark of the night, I made my escape to a safe house.

The twenty-two, however, were held for two days at the police station while the police issued a warrant for my arrest. It became obvious that despite infringing on their rights, the police would hold them as hostages until such time as I surrendered. When I voluntarily availed myself to the police on the third day, we were all promptly arraigned in court before armed police and a huge crowd of media.

However, we were denied bail, as we were considered a danger to the peace. The court ordered us to be taken to the same Kitale Prison for the weekend and to return to court on Monday when a ruling would be made on our case. After spending a long weekend as guests of the government in Kitale Prison we were eventually granted cash bail and told we had to answer to charges of malicious damage, unlawful assembly, and in my case an additional charge of incitement to violence since I was deemed responsible as the organizer of the protest. The latter charge had a maximum life sentence attached to it.

The three nights in Kitale Prison was a very chastening experience. We arrived after dark from court and were frogmarched to the cells. The Officer in Charge, Mr Julius Odera, had mercy on me. I was given a tiny cell with two other seniors although we had to share two tiny one-inch mattresses on a very uneven and damp surface for three nights. Odera had his good wife prepare tea, eggs and bread for us before sleeping as we had not eaten the whole day. For the rest of our stay, we survived on green cabbage and half cooked porridge. On Sunday, I led the prison church service to the delight of one prisoner who announced that now I was really one of them. On Monday morning the others were taken to court. I was left behind to await the court's ruling as I was considered a security threat as crowds would throng the court to witness proceedings.

47

It was an anxious and lonely ten hours waiting for the verdict to come from the court. At least I had the cell to myself as my companions had gone to court. For the prison warders who started their week's duty on Monday I was a bit of a novelty as they kept continuously peeping through the tiny cell bars and inquiring for my welfare. Eventually, late in the evening, one of our advocates arrived from court and delivered the ruling that I had been granted surety and should be released immediately.

I missed the opportunity to celebrate that moment with my comrades who had gone home directly from the courts. It was a strange feeling to be able to put on my shoes and watch again and to know the time. I rushed home and immediately enjoyed the simple pleasure of a much-needed hot shower.

However, by then the issue had acquired international media attention[28] and this caused embarrassment to the Kenyan Government as it confirmed suspicions about the extent of the looting of public resources in Kenya.[29] Even back in my home county of Fermanagh, local councillor Bernice Swift protested the arrests of the twenty-three and the wholesale grabbing of land in Kenya.

The case against us never took off as a question raised in Parliament to the Minister of Lands regarding the ownership of the disputed park confirmed that it was indeed public land. The complainant had no right to demand redress and so we all walked free. Eventually the government had acknowledged that Kitale Park was public land. Kitale Park was just one of the many pieces of land we wanted repossessed and secured.

The land campaign was a most worthy and popular one. It also inspired many others to take up the challenge of repossessing public land elsewhere. One of the most memorable and committed public officers we engaged with in that respect was Kitale Prison boss, Hussein Rashid. In 2005 with a little practical support from CJPC he took back a ten-acre plot at Kitale Remand Prison that had been utilized by county councillors for years. Rashid devised a secret plan to repossess it and I became a willing collaborator.

---

28 http://demokrasia-kenya.blogspot.com/2005/08/free-father-dolan-and-his-23-fellow.html

29 https://www.breakingnews.ie/ireland/priest-arrested-at-kenya-land-rights-demo-215892.html

At 4am two tractors arrived at the prison gates, fuelled and fitted with ploughs. Rashid woke up all the prisoners and ordered them to remove the illegal fencing on the disputed land and leave it in a secure place for its owners. The ten acres were all ploughed before the grabbers woke up. Rather basic fencing was mounted and soon after maize seed was planted by the inmates. There was not a murmur from the aggrieved political class. After being promoted to take charge of the much larger Kitale Farm Prison, Rashid was able to take possession of much of their lost agricultural land in 2010.[30] Sadly he passed away in January 2017 and was buried in the Muslim Cemetery in Eldoret.

More progress was made when James Orengo was lands minister. He also repossessed Mount Elgon Hospital and Kitale Academy School which had been taken over by a local tycoon, Nathaniel Tum, MD of Kenya Seed Company and a point man for Moi in Kitale for decades. Regarding the hospital, Mr Orengo said 'This has always been a public institution managed by a trust comprised of the municipal and county councils who later breeched the trusteeship by turning it into a private liability company and proceeding to take loans against the public property. I order the Title to be issued to Permanent Secretary and the facility to be run by the Ministry of Medical Services'.[31] Orengo also recovered the 43 acres of Kitale Academy School a part of which had been grabbed by the same individual.

However, there remains much more land to be reclaimed. My only regret over this entire affair is that those entrusted with continuing the land campaign chose to handle less sensitive matters when I left Kitale in 2006. Still the seed was planted and there is a time for everything as the Bible says.

30   https://www.standardmedia.co.ke/article/2000021665/top-officials-surrender-prison-land
31   Saturday Nation, February 20, 2010

Fury over assault on priest

PICTURES: COURTESY KTN AND JACOB OTIENO

Picture 1, Father Gabriel Dolan displays the envelope containing grievances he intended to present to Vice-President Moody Awori. Pictures 2-5, an officer grabs the priest by the trouser and forcefully drags him into a waiting police car. In picture 6, the pri est is seen gesticulating as he protests the police treatment. Picture 7 shows human rights activists demonstrating in Nairobi yesterday against the arrest of Fr Dolan.

Celebration with Kitale 23 charged with illegal assembly and destruction of property

Handing over gifts to Prisoners in Kitale Prison July 2006

Celebration with Kitale 23 charged with illegal assembly and destruction of property

Celebration with Kitale 23 charged with illegal assembly and destruction of property

24   THE PEOPLE DAILY, Saturday, November 8, 2003

THE PEOPLE TELEPHONE NUMBERS
350584, 253166, 253423, 253168, 249686, 253304
Mobile lines: 0733-833612, 0722-359493
FOR OUR COAST READERS.
Please Call 011-220646

PEOPLE
Fair, Frank and Fearless   **Daily**

POSTAL ADDRESS

To Write to
THE PEOPLE DAILY
Please use the following address
The People Limited
P.O. Box 10296
00100 - Nairobi

Catholic Church demands the release of Father G. Dolan

By JOSEPHINE MWANGI and DANE MWIRIGI

THE Catholic Church and several human rights organisations yesterday roundly condemned the manhandling and arrest by police of Father Gabriel Dolan in Kitale on Thursday. They demanded for the unconditional release of Fr Golan failure to which they would go to the streets to demand for the same.

Addressing a press conference at Holy Family Basilica, Nairobi, the groups also demanded for the sacking of commissioner of Prisons Abraham Kamakil who they alleged is the beneficiary of the grabbed land.

They challenged President Mwai Kibaki to move fast and rid his government of corrupt officers from the former Kanu regime who they accused of being behind "such shameful acts".

The priest was arrested together with activists Boniface Wanyoike, Thomas Kariuki and Patrick Kirito while leading a delegation to present a petition on land grabbing to vice president Moody Awori who was visiting the area.

Among the organisations represented at the press conference were Catholic Justice Peace Commission (CJPC), Kenya Human Rights Commission (KHRC), People Against Torture, Litigation Fund Against Torture, Operation Firimbi and Independent Medico-Legal Unit.

Fr Dolan is the co-ordinator of the Kitale Peace and Justice Commission, which has been at the forefront in speaking against land grabbing in the region.

And in a statement, the Kenya National Commission on Human Rights termed the manhandling of the priest

Members of civil society - Operation Firimbi, Catholic Justice Peace Commission, Kenya Human Rights Commission, among others, yesterday demonstrated at Holy Family Basilica against the arrest of Fr Gabriel Dolan and two others in Kitale over the grabbing of government land by top government officials - FELIX OBUNA

before the cameras as unfortunate and uncalled for. "This incident is

symptomatic of the brutality with which the police continue to relate with Kenyans," a

statement signed by the commission's vice chairperson Violet Mavisi read in part.

The commission called upon the minister for national security Dr Chris Murungaru and police commissioner Edwin Nyaseda to take firm action against the police officers who manhandled Fr Dolan.

It also called upon the ministry of home affairs to look into allegations of grabbing of prison land that Fr Dolan and his team were attempting to bring to the fore before they were humiliatingly arrested.

The organisations addressing the press at Holy Family called on President Mwai Kibaki to sack the beneficiaries of the grabbed land who they said had influenced the arrest and assault on Fr Dolan.

They also called for the sacking of the police officer captured on live television footage dragging the priest to the police car. The action, they said, amounted to violation of human rights.

Church attacks Wako over Akiwumi report

The Sunday Standard 29/06/03

By Hilton Otenyo

minister for lands and human settlements Amos Kimunya looks at a petition brough[t] by Father Gabriel Dolan, the director Catholic Justce Peace and Commission Kitale, af[ter pre]senting complaints of land grabbing to the minister at his Ardhi House office yesterd[ay]
IAN NYAMBURA

The People 26/06/03

ATTORNEY-GENERAL Amos Wako yesterday came under a scathing attack from the Catholic Church for failing to prosecute people who were named in the Akiwumi Report on the 1992 tribal clashes.

The Catholic Justice and Peace Commission (CJPC) also asked Kanu Secretary-General Julius Sunkuli to disqualify himself from the task force on the establishment of a truth and reconcilliation commission because he had been named in the Akiwumi Report.

Kitale CJPC Co-ordinator Father Gabriel Dolan said that even if the commission was formed, its reports would not be acted upon as long as Wako was still the A-G as he would still frustrate their implementation.

"One reason is that when the Akiwumi Report was released to the public three years ago, Wako dismissed it and issued a rejoinder defending the culprits, who included Sunkuli," said Dolan.

Dolan said the Narc Government should act on the report by prosecuting prominent politicians who played leading roles in the clashes.

Dolan made the remarks in a memorandum he presented to the task force on establishment of TRC during its sitting at the Kakamega County Hall.

He said Kenyans do not need another commission to repeat what was already known.

Dolan said the church was taking care of 150 families who

WAKO: **Criticised**

were displaced by the clashes in Trans Nzoia district. He said the families require justice by being compensated by the Government.

Dolan said that by calling for TRC, it was implying that the truth is not known or there is widespread disagreement about the truth of recent history.

He said the problem that led to rampant injustice in Kenya was the disregard of the constitution by the former regimes.

He said once the ring leaders were removed from the way now that they are known, it will make it easier for the low-key players of injustice to come forward to ask for forgiveness and make it safer for them to tell the truth.

Dolan said Wako's retirement will pave way for investigations and prosecution of culprits of injustice to Kenyans.

6

WHEN A WHOLE COMMUNITY IS DEMONISED

The Pokot community has probably been the most vilified and demonised ethnic group in Kenyan history. Regarded as belligerent, hostile to outsiders and unfriendly to any of their neighbours, they rarely got sympathy in times of difficulty while, truth be told, their so-called spokespersons did little to rectify that image in the public eye over the years.

Francis Lotodo was the self-appointed king of the community for over two decades. There was no room for any other voice to emerge to express the real community needs or aspirations. The entire government machinery obeyed every instruction that he decreed because he represented Baba Moi in the District. So, when Lotodo spoke, President Moi was speaking and you promptly obeyed.

Lotodo of course played a pivotal role in the ethnic clashes that occurred prior to the 1992 elections. Farmers and businessmen were burned out and banished forever from his Kapenguria constituency. This ethnic violence just fed and reinforced the public perception that the Pokot were warmongers and cattle rustlers, with little respect for any law bar that of the jungle.

Part of the CJPC strategy in West Pokot was to confront and expose the system that kept the district a closed, isolated and impoverished one, and to also give room for the Pokot to voice their own concerns about matters of development and marginalisation. That was a tough mandate as even renowned and respected voices like Gibson Kamau Kuria expressed their frustrations and prejudices by calling the community secessionists and tribalists, not committed to any real development.

In a rejoinder that was published in Sunday Nation of February 7, 1999 I challenged Kuria to be better informed on how the community had been marginalised and exploited by the KANU regime, and suggested that it was no surprise that some members of the community invested in an AK47 when there was no other option left for them to gain a living. KANU was a cover and justification for exploiting the community and Lotodo, far from being an asset to the community, conspired by his silence with the Moi Mafia to exploit the few resources available in the District to impoverish and alienate the residents.

The first betrayal of course was regarding the construction of the infamous Turkwell Gorge Hydroelectric Dam. This project went ahead despite the warnings that came from an international Environmental Impact Assessment (EIA) study undertaken by the Norwegian company, Norconsult. The dam is expected to dry up in two years' time, and even if that does not occur, it is built on a fault line that may crack any time and flood the communities downstream.[32]

The project was the brainchild and creation of Nicholas Biwott, a powerful man in the Moi administration, who ignored the professional advice and proceeded to implement with gusto after he had himself appointed as Minister of Energy. In one of the many corrupt deals associated with the powerful minister, the dam was overpriced by $300 million. At its inception in 1986 it was estimated to cost $150 million. However, the contract was single-sourced and when granted to the French Company Spie Batignolles the cost had jumped to $250 million. The final cost was a whopping $450 million.

The European Delegate at the time, Achim Kratz, claimed that millions of dollars were paid into the private accounts of Biwott and Moi by the French contractor Spie Batignolles.[33] Many more details of this deal can be found in Wikileaks in the section entitled "The looting of Kenya under President Moi".[34]

However, Lotodo never raised a single complaint about the dam project in parliament nor did he pursue promises made by Biwott and the construction company that the Pokot community would be compensated for the loss of their land, grazing sources and access to water points. His silence most likely had its own price. There were even agreements to the effect that 22,000 acres would be irrigated downstream but thirty years later that has become another broken promise.

But most extraordinary of all was that all the electricity generated at the Turkwell Gorge was transferred directly to the National Grid at Lessos, Eldoret, two hundred kilometres away. Neither Turkana nor Pokot legislators demanded that their communities should benefit from the power. At the time, no town in Turkana was connected to the national grid and it was only Kapenguria and, wait for it, the home of Lotodo in Parua eight kilometres away that received mains electricity. That did

---

32   https://www.nation.co.ke/news/politics/Turkwel-Dam--Biwott-pet-project/1064-5507432-130s3mfz/index.html

33   https://www.theelephant.info/features/2019/09/05/tales-of-state-capture-goldenberg-anglo-leasing-and-eurobond/

34   https://wikileaks.org/wiki/The_looting_of_Kenya_under_President_Moi

not seem to bother anyone and just confirmed prejudices that the Pokot were not the slightest bit interested in modern development.

That was our motivation and entry point in launching a campaign demanding that the communities of Turkana and Pokot should be connected to the national grid as it would greatly enhance the potential of the local people to develop themselves and their industries and services. Extraordinarily, most MPs laughed at the proposal, claiming that both communities were pastoralists and did not need electricity to mind their animals. Some even suggested that they only needed guns and bullets to protect themselves. In fact, I know one particular MP who always enticed people to vote for him by distributing bullets during campaign time, a commodity that he reckoned was much more popular and valuable than basic foodstuffs.

We produced IEC (Information, Education and Communication) materials on the subject matter with the message that while both communities fought over a few half-starved goats, over their heads the real wealth was being transferred to the highlands of Kenya. Put another way, how long would they choose to remain in poverty and in the dark while their light was benefiting other communities? The research that we published was entitled, 'Turkwell Gorge – A real opportunity to transform the Pokot-Turkana conflict'.

Thanks to extraordinary efforts of Lucas Aryong in the Kainuk office of CJPC and his counterpart Samuel Lemali in Sigor, this message reached the masses and got people thinking. Folk began to realise that they had much more in common, namely POVERTY, than what divided them and as long as they fought each other this endemic poverty would remain. That was real civic education, focused on changing attitudes and bringing visible improvement to the lives of the people. It represented a complete overhaul and reversal of community thinking and values. It was indeed possible to live differently and in harmony with one's neighbours.

It took more than a few years for Kenya Power to heed the many requests and demands made for access to electricity but most small towns nearby like Kainuk, Sigor, Ortum, Sarimach and Chepareria were eventually connected to the national grid. But it took almost twenty years for that to happen. Of course, this did not immediately solve the issue of conflict along the mutual borders, but it did represent a different approach to what the communities really needed and deserved just like every other Kenyan community. If it did not resolve the conflict it was in fact a real attempt at transforming it. It also aspired to bring the communities into the twenty-first century and take their places as citizens of the Republic of Kenya.

The other great natural asset that God had endowed the Pokot community with was an abundance of limestone in the Sebit area of Ortum. Yet for three decades the potential to transform the economic conditions of the local people has yet to be developed. This is due to a poisonous cocktail of appalling leadership and political corruption.

The first company to recognise the potential of the area was Kavee Quarries from Mombasa who, under the protection of Sigor MP Christopher Lomada, bought up the land for a pittance from the local peasants in the 1980s. The community had no idea of the real value of their assets and Lomada did nothing to enlighten them. Their schools received a few sheets of mabati roofing and a few cartons of exercise books that were expected to ensure their cooperation in the name of corporate social responsibility (CSR). Most of these issues were captured in an Op-Ed piece I contributed to the Daily Nation of May 3, 2006.[35]

Kavee Quarries never kept their promise to build a cement factory but instead transported the limestone by road to the factory of Tororo Cement in Uganda. This outright rape of the resources was brought to an abrupt end in 1999 when university students from Pokot and CJPC officials physically prevented the transportation in an incident that also saw one lorry of Kavee Quarries burnt to cinders. Kavee Quarries however, did not give up and after once more 'persuading' another set of local politicians and the provincial administration they resumed the transportation to Uganda in 2002. By now, however, the community were fully aware of the potential of the hidden wealth in their midst.

Research done by CJPC with an Irish cement company, Quinn Cement, revealed that there was 22 million tons of limestone in the area that could produce six million bags of cement each year for the next half century. Equipped with this knowledge, David Pkosing and the university students once more stopped the transportation despite the desperate pleas on behalf of Kavee by Regional Development Minister, Musikari Kombo[36] and the local District Commissioner. It was pretty clear that there were certain advantages and benefits to their favoured position as neither Kavee nor the government ever presented any architectural plans for constructing the factory.

---

35   https://www.nation.co.ke/oped/1192-121296-l7jnds/index.html

36   Daily Nation, May 5th 2004

Kavee Quarries eventually pulled out of the County in 2006 citing frustrations in acquiring electricity power as the excuse for their failure to construct the cement factory. Then negotiations began with other prospectors and an Indian company, Cemtech was identified in 2009 as the new investor. They promised the creation of 1,200 jobs for the local community after the factory began operations[37] but despite promises and programmes they never got operations going. It looked like another fraudulent agreement between dubious businesses and corrupt politicians from the locality.

The asset has recently changed hands for a third time with a Tanzanian company, Simba Cement, taking over in September 2019 with the promise that by late 2020 the factory would be fully operational.[38] Mining Minister John Munyes cancelled the licence of Cemtech and gave it to Simba late last year. Two decades have been lost in the factory's production and to date there has been no tangible benefit to the local Pokot community due to massive corruption and petty, selfish politicians who put their own greed before the needs and rights of their constituents. Regretfully, similar occurrences have been replicated all over the country and at national level, where corruption stifles the spirit of entrepreneurship and opportunities for development of the nation.

One further contribution towards the exposure and enhancement of the rights of the Pokot community that is worth mentioning was the community's participation in the Constitution of Kenya Review Commission (CKRC) under the chairmanship of Professor Yash Pal Ghai. For decades the community had made frequent and aggressive claims about land in Trans Nzoia that they claimed had been forcefully occupied by the colonial administration in the early twentieth century when the community was driven back into the arid, harsh lands that they currently occupy. These assertions caused considerable tension along the common border with Trans Nzoia for several years.

To reduce the heat around the matter and to shed more light on the legitimacy of their claims we undertook a study of several months including visits to the land registry and the national archives as we attempted to discover the historical roots of the community's alleged grievances. In April 2002, CJPC and Kenya Land Alliance (KLA) Coordinator, Odenda Lumumba, facilitated the community's presentation to

---

37   http://htl.li/PXjBh

38   https://www.businessdailyafrica.com/economy/Simba-Cement-Pokot-plant-work-to-de lay/3946234-5266738-e8twm9z/index.html

Professor Ghai while dozens of the community representatives also attended in traditional attire.

They received a lot of attention in both print and electronic media and the community were very pleasantly surprised that Kenyans were ready to pay attention to their grievances. This exercise showed that there was a peaceful and rational way to present their concerns and in participating in the CKRC process they took their rightful place alongside other Kenyan communities which also had been marginalised and discriminated against for decades.

The 2010 Constitution devoted an entire chapter to land and natural resources and recommended a structure to address historical land injustices. To date the government has ignored that recommendation alongside many others. Yet the Maasai, Pokot, Ogiek and many other communities have long memories and have not forgotten the land injustices and suffering that affect them until today. The communities may no longer be demonised but until such time as they get a meaningful hearing and redress, they will continue to feel alienated from the Kenyan state.

Devolution has greatly enhanced the County of Pokot and given the people confidence, jobs and investment. Our little efforts at transforming the agenda and opportunities for the Pokot people may have contributed to prepare a platform for devolution to take root and to enhance public participation in its programmes. But it will take a lot more to ensure that they are given their rightful place at the decision-making table in Kenya. That may take another generation of advocacy.

7

THE DEMISE OF BETT AND THE FALL
FROM GRACE OF KIRWA

Trans Nzoia has been a political hot bed for decades due to its cosmopolitan make-up and the fact that the area has produced two very nationally minded opposition leaders in the persons of the late Masinde Muliro and Kijana Wamalwa. Yet the most controversial politician to emerge in the 1990s was the firebrand Kipruto arap Kirwa, who represented Cherangany constituency for the best part of two decades.

Kirwa was a member of the ruling party, KANU, but only in name. He was rebellious, provocative and determined to represent the interests of his constituents who were a mixture of half a dozen ethnic groups in the richly agricultural constituency. Moi had little time for the opposition but even less for dissenting voices within his own ruling party. They were expected to toe the line and if they objected, they were either rigged out of office or bought off with parcels of public land.

Kirwa did not succumb to either the stick or carrot option. He remained ruthlessly independent, bold and questioning from within. As a result, he was loved by his constituents and despised by the KANU elites. Moi then attempted to silence and subdue him within his own constituency and used the provincial administration and the police force as the means to break his influence. The District Commissioner, who was most subservient as regards orders from the executive, was Samuel Oreta.

The harassment and intimidation of Kirwa began around the turn of the century. A funds drive in Kaplamai division was brutally attacked by administration police under the supervision of local chief, Michael Arusei, in November 2000. Two weeks later I was present to witness riot police take over Kipkeikei Secondary School where Kirwa was scheduled to oversee another funds drive for the school dormitory. When I spotted the few dozen officers charge into the compound, I grabbed Kirwa's wrist and rushed into a classroom. By the time the police caught up with us, we were on our knees, praying fervently for safety and refuge.

The police raged into the classroom but were stunned to silence as I led the prayers. Some even removed their helmets as we continued. The prayer exercise lasted about five minutes and then the police ordered us to leave the school and disperse the crowd, which we duly did.[39] However, we walked out of the school with a sense of victory and defiance for the symbolic gesture had not been in vain. There would be many more such struggles and disruption in the coming months as the government did not give any indication that they would cease the harassment.

Matters came to a head with the killing of a very close ally of Kirwa, David Bett, a former councillor in the area, just after Christmas 2000. Bett lived in Kaplamai and a series of events in which I was involved made me wonder if in fact I could also have been the initial target of the assassination.

It all began on the evening of Christmas Eve when I went to celebrate Mass with the Christian community of Kaplamai in Cherangany constituency. After the service, the catechist gave me an envelope addressed to me that had been hand delivered that afternoon. The unsigned letter claimed that the author was a police informer in Nairobi. He said that he had been in a certain Nairobi police station and heard police officers discussing how Fr John Kaiser had been murdered. He claimed that he had all the details of the priest's death and he wanted to share that information with me before he returned to Nairobi after the Christmas holidays. He furthermore asked to meet me the following day and said I should confirm my willingness to come through the catechist.

It was now late so I relayed the message that I could not meet on Christmas Day but that he should come on the following day and meet at the church at 2pm. I also requested the catechist to come and identify the man, although he had not known the same person prior to being handed the envelope. We waited outside the church under a tree and soon the catechist pointed out the man while he was still a few hundred metres away. I already began to feel dread and anxiety about this person. My instinct and my guardian angel were warning me to tread very cautiously.

When he arrived, I insisted that we meet in the open ground outside the church as I felt safer that way. He repeated his claims, adding that he had another colleague who was in the police station that particular night and that he would like us to go and meet him together in my vehicle. I listened for a few minutes and then incensed uttered these few harsh words, 'Who sent you? Why do you want to kill me? Get out of here fast before I attack you'. He was startled, clearly not expecting such an angry reaction. He took off in a hurry without saying a word. I threw dust after him and drove home at great speed.

---

39   Daily Nation, November 26th 2000

That night David Bett was assassinated in his home, some three hundred metres away from Kaplamai Catholic church. I was devastated. Later the next day, I went to condole with the family and discovered more about his killing. The family of the late Bett were together when a group of armed men broke into the home. They asked which one was David Bett and proceeded to pump bullets into him. His nephew was also shot dead as he resisted the assault. Nothing was stolen from the home. The gang left immediately after the killing, taking Bett's vehicle but abandoning it later. His was clearly a targeted killing and not a result of armed robbery.[40] The police took three hours to arrive at the scene although their base at Kachibora was just a few kilometres away.

Christmas is a quiet time in the media houses. All the local stringers had gone to their rural homes. I prepared a statement that was faxed to the Eldoret media houses demanding that the police investigate his killing as a matter of urgency since it appeared like a targeted assassination. It created a furore as the Criminal Investigation Department (CID) boss in Kitale went public and stated that they wanted me to record a statement on whatever I knew about his death.

It appeared like a warrant for my arrest. However, after contacting my advocate, Jeremiah Samba, we went to the police headquarters in Kitale to respond to their demand. The police maintained that they would record my statement. I, however, insisted that I would write my own since I had gone to school and knew how to write. This jostling went on for more than half an hour until the CID Boss, Sammy Mukeku, eventually conceded ground and I proceeded to write my statement and sign it. I then left town for a few days to avoid any tension that might arise around Mr Bett's burial.

For the record, President Moi attended the funeral. He had also attended the burial of the assassinated Foreign Minister, Robert Ouko in 1990.

Five men were arrested and charged for the murder of Bett in mid-January 2001. They were denied bail and kept on remand at Kitale Farm Prison. They were due in court in February of the same year but never arrived there. As the Prison lorry transporting them slowed down crossing the road bumps in the Kitale outskirts, they all jumped off and escaped, never to be found. The armed prison wardens did nothing to prevent their escape. To date no one can tell who murdered Bett, or why, but suspicions understandably remain.

---

40   https://allafrica.com/stories/200012280105.html and Daily Nation December 28th 2000

But even afterwards, Kirwa continued to have his meetings disrupted by state security officials. Moi never relented in his assaults and directed Ministers Henry Kosgey, Julius Sunkuli, Nicholas Biwott and Assistant Minister William Ruto to hold harambee (fundraising) meetings in Cherangany in a move intended to undermine Kirwa.[41] All of the aforementioned were adversely mentioned as being ringleaders of the politically motivated land clashes in the previous decade.

In a move reminiscent of those dreaded land clashes of 1997, the fundraising activities of the Moi Cabinet were quickly followed by the printing of leaflets warning members of the Kisii community to vacate their farms and homes in Cherangany or be burned out[42]. This was clearly designed as a further threat to discredit Kirwa's leadership and his supporters and a confirmation of how dangerous the Moi regime really was. For the record the Kisii generally gave their votes to Kirwa.

When we at CJPC demanded an investigation into the source of the leaflets, KANU leaders in Trans Nzoia repeated the familiar call for my deportation. In July of the same year, I received an unsigned letter in the post with a death threat as the contents. Although I reported the matter to the police, no action was taken despite the fact that Trans Nzoia councillor, Pius Kauka, had been earlier reported to have uttered similar threats in public.[43] Whatever the sources of the threats, they were clearly sanctioned by the state machinery.

Still, Kirwa continued with his activities, undaunted by the many threats that came his way. He decamped from KANU and joined the party of NARC led by Mwai Kibaki. He romped home to an easy victory in the 2002 General Election and was rewarded with the post of Agricultural Minister in the new government.

We had few dealings with him after that. Only one is worthy of mention. After being informed that tractors belonging to the state-owned Agricultural Development Corporation (ADC) were ploughing the farm of Kirwa at the start of the planting season in 2003, I asked to meet him. We had a very brief early morning cup of tea at Kitale Club one Sunday morning. When I questioned him about the same, he replied that he did not have anything to do with the farm as his wife handles all his business affairs. I quickly drank my cup of tea and proceeded to church.

---

41   Daily Nation, February 10,2001

42   The People, March 7, 2001

43   Daily Nation, July 19, 2001

His faulty explanation spoke volume
and we have not met since that day
Despite the excitement that the K
baki government produced afte
their election, the honeymoon per
od was short-lived as they failed t
meet the expectations of the Ker
yan public. Kirwa in particular faile
to bring much needed reform to th
agricultural sector. In recent genera
elections he has failed to get electe
either as an MP or a Senator in suc
cessive ballots.

Yet there was no regret about ou
commitment to monitor and highligh
his harassment in those times; di:
appointment at his failure to delive
but no regret about standing for wha
was right at the time.

**Priest quizzed over
murder statement**
Daily Nation 3/01/2007

Catholic cleric is quizzed on killing

By GEORGE OMONSO
and VINCENT BARTOO

Police have questioned Kitale Catholic priest Gabriel Dolan over his claims on the murder of Mr David Bett, said to be Kanu MP Kipruto Kirwa's ally.

Accompanied by his lawyer, Mr Jeremiah Samba, the priest recorded statements over his claims that Mr Bett had been assassinated.

Father Dolan asked why the police used the Press to make contact with him, yet he lives in Kitale.

"I have not gone into hiding. Why did the police appeal for my statement through the Press?" he asked.

The clergyman denied suggestions that his claims were alarmist, adding that everyone was free to voice concern over the murder.

"As a human rights defender, I was addressing the legitimate fears of the local people. Is it criminal for people to be suspicious, especially when there are grounds for such suspicion?" Fr Dolan asked.

The Trans-Nzoia CID boss, Mr Sammy Mukeku, was on Saturday quoted in the Press as saying the police were looking for the priest to record a statement.

Addressing mourners at Mr Bett's funeral on Monday, Trans Nzoia District Commissioner Samuel Oreta said that seven suspects have so far been arrested in connection with the murder of Mr Bett and his nephew Aaron.

Police were pursuing more suspects believed to have fled into the neighbouring Bungoma District.

Meanwhile, Mr Kirwa, the Cherangany MP, failed to address mourners during Mr Bett's burial.

During a harambee in aid of Mr Bett's family, Mr Kirwa donated Sh30,000, but made no effort to address the gathering.

The function was on Torongo Farm, Kaplamai Division, in his constituency.

The MP sat on the periphery of the main podium, occupied mainly by his political rivals.

Those who sat on the main dais included nominated MP Zipporah Kittony, Assistant Minister Musa Sirma, African Inland Church assistant Bishop Silas Yego and the Trans Nzoia District Commissioner, Mr Samuel Oreta.

Also present were Industrial Bank chairman Reuben Chesire, the chairman of the Cherangany Development Support Group, Mr William Sawe, the group's secretary, Mr Yusuf Chepkole, Cllr William Chesire and retired Army commander Augustine Cheruiyot.

Armed police in plainclothes under Kitale commandant Alfred Ngetich patrolled the venue, following claims that some of Mr Kirwa's supporters had threatened to cause chaos.

Youths opposed to Mr Kirwa, led by Mr Noor Kirwa, also patrolled the farm.

Before the harambee started, the Rev Yego conducted a short prayer and then the master of ceremonies, Cherangani District Officer James Murungi, invited Mr Bett's son to speak. He denied that his father had ever associated himself with Mr Kirwa.

Of all the invited guests, only Mr Sirma acknowledged Mr Kirwa's presence.

Mr Oreta, who has been accused of using the provincial administration to cancel Mr Kirwa's public meetings, ignored the MP's presence.

Later, Mr Kirwa told the *Nation* that he had attended the harambee because Mr Bett was not only his constituent but also a neighbour and friend.

"I did not come here to meet fellow leaders, but to pay my last respects to my friend Bett."

Some Sh306,000 was raised.

63

Probe threat to kill priest, urges Kirwa

By GEORGE OMONSO

The government has been asked to investigate threats made against two Catholic priests.

Cherangany MP Kipruto arap Kirwa said threats to kill Fr Gabriel Dolan of the Kitale Catholic Justice and Peace Commission and eviction of his Mokwa Parish counterpart, Fr Michael Rop, should not be taken lightly.

Mr Kirwa said the government should arrest a nominated councillor, Mr Pius Mzee arap Kauka, who threatened to lead Sabaot youths in "killing" Fr Dolan over a disputed 2000-acre farm in Trans Nzoia.

Fr Dolan has been advocating that squatters and victims of tribal clashes be settled on the land formerly known as John Smith Farm. Some of the squatters were evicted from Kiboroa Forest in 1987.

The disputed farm is owned by Kokwo co-operative society.

Speaking to the Press at his Cherangany home, Mr Kirwa said the threats against Fr Dolan and Fr Rop are part of a to intimidate Catholic priests engaged in civic education.

He said the government was opposed

to civic education ahead of next year's General Election.

Mr Kirwa defended Fr Dolan saying the priest has been fighting for the rights of the poor in the North Rift.

The MP said Mr Kauka was a frequent visitor to State House and his threats should not be taken lightly.

Mr Kirwa said the chairman of the constitutional review process Prof Yash Pal Ghai should give a regular briefing to the public on the progress of his team.

Such briefings, he said, would shape public contributions to the review team.

"We don't know what they are doing, when they expect to hand in the report and what will happen if the process goes beyond 2002."

The MP said it was also important for Prof Ghai as the chairman of the review process to suggest ways through which government critics can interact with the public, given police hostility to public rallies.

He said ignoring such issues could contribute to a lopsided constitutional process where the majority of Kenyans would not air their views.

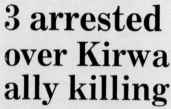

Mr Kirwa: Call

---

3 arrested over Kirwa ally killing

Daily Nation 29/12/2000

Meanwhile, Mr Kirwa's angry supporters yesterday said they feared for Kirwa's life and called for his protection by the government and the international human rights community.

Speaking to the Press in Kitale, the MP's supporters led by councillor David Osoro, Mr Vincent Rono and John Bitok Boit, said the murders of Mr Bett's and his nephew Aaron were signs that the MP was in danger.

They said Mr Kirwa's meetings have been disrupted by youths and the police under the pretext that they were illegal.

They said they supported Fr Gabriel Dolan, the Kitale co-coordinator of the Catholic Justice and Peace Commission, who said that the killing was a planned assassination meant to scare the MP and his supporters.

The Cherangany residents also told Police Commissioner Philemon Abong'o to explain why it took the police three hours to arrive at the murder scene despite the fact that Kachibora police station is only three kilometres away.

Meanwhile, assistant minister Musa Sirma yesterday called for thorough investigations into Mr Bett's killing.

Mr Sirma, who condemned the killing however, cautioned politicians and church leaders against politicising the matter.

Daily Nation 30/12/2000

Two more held over killing

By NATION Correspondent

Two more suspects have been arrested over the killing of Mr David Bett, Cherangany MP Kipruto Kirwa's political ally.

At the same time, the Tugen community in Cherangany has denied that the man was ever an associate of Mr Kirwa.

The two bring to five the number of suspects being interrogated over the murder of Mr Bett and his nephew Aaron Bett at his Torongo farm in Kaplamai, Cherangany.

The Trans Nzoia crime boss, Mr Sammy Mukeku, said the police are looking for Father Gabriel Dolan, the director of the Kitale Catholic Diocese Peace and Justice Commission, to record a statement over his claims that Mr Bett was assassinated.

The Standard 28/12/2000

After learning of the incident, the Catholic Justice and Peace Commission, Kitale Chapter Director, Father Gabriel Dolan, called for the arrest and prosecution of the suspects "to dispel fears that this was political."

But the Cherangani Kanu Sub-branch Secretary, Mr Yusuf Chepkole, warned the Catholic Church against politicising the incident and said it should be left to the police to investigate."

The Standard 30/12/2000

Trans Nzoia Kanu leaders, however, asked the Government to investigate claims by a Kitale Catholic priest, Father Gabriel Dolan, that the killings had been planned.

Messrs Chepkole, Francis Rono and Coun Pius Mzee Arap Kauka termed Father Dolan's claim serious and demanded that they be fully investigated.

8

WHO KILLED JOHN KAISER?

✝

On the morning of August 23 2000, Kenyans woke to the news that the shattered body of Fr John Anthony Kaiser had been found on the roadside near Naivasha turn-off on the main Nakuru–Nairobi highway. Kaiser was a Mill Hill Missionary from Minnesota, USA, who first came to Kenya after his ordination as a priest in 1964.

After spending many years in the Diocese of Kisii in Western Kenya, he was appointed to the Diocese of Ngong in 1993, with the specific ministry of being chaplain to the displaced people in Maela camp who had been forcefully and violently removed from their homes and farms by armed political gangs. He did exceptional work tending to their every need and became the unofficial spokesman of these thousands of afflicted Kenyans. However, the camp was forcefully closed by the Kenyan government overnight in December 1994, despite his loud protests.

Still, the determined and extremely organised priest had documented the abuses meted out on the internally displaced as well as investigating the political involvement in orchestrating the violence and forced displacement of the people. When the government established a Commission of Inquiry into what they deemed merely land clashes, John Kaiser had all his evidence at hand and presented it in Nakuru in 1998. The Commission was popularly known as the Akiwumi Commission after its Chair, a Ghanaian Judge attached to the Kenyan Judiciary.

The Commission of Inquiry however were flabbergasted when the burly priest publicly named President Daniel arap Moi and energy Minister Nicholas Biwott as the principal architects in what he considered politically instigated ethnic land clashes. No other witness had been so daring as to point the finger at the Head of State who by then had been in office for two decades.

The Commission however, for reasons never made known to the public, chose to expunge Fr Kaiser's evidence from its final report which was eventually handed over after many delays in October 2002 to Mr Moi. However, by then Fr Kaiser's claims and evidence were already in the public domain and that made him a legitimate target of the Moi regime whom the public generally blamed for the assassination of Foreign Minister Robert Ouko in 1990. Assassinations and disappearances were nothing new in this era so the government would almost certainly be suspect number one.

Furthermore, Fr Kaiser had in 1999 made another enemy in the person of Minister Julius Sunkuli whom he accused of raping teenage Maasai girls. Again, Kaiser was meticulous in his documentation and submitted all the evidence to the Federation of Women Lawyers, Nairobi (FIDA). When his body was found that cold August morning, there was no shortage of suspects among the political elite and the nation's power brokers. One of the girls, Florence Maipei, withdrew her allegations one week after Fr Kaiser was assassinated.

I was in Ireland when John Kaiser was assassinated and returned to Nairobi a few days after his burial. However, upon arrival I was informed by my colleagues in our St Patrick's Society leadership house that our community was hosting the catechist of John Kaiser, Mr Francis Kantai. We had been requested to do so by a Loreto Sister, a friend of Fr Kaiser, Nuala Brannigan. Due to my experience in human rights, I was requested to meet Kantai and to assess how we might best be of assistance to him since he was concerned that his life was also in danger. He had not even dared to attend the burial service in Lolgorian, his home parish.

I had not met Kantai previously but was familiar with him through experiences shared with the same Sister. Indeed, I had only met John Kaiser rather briefly in 1999 when he sought refuge in the same St Patrick's house at a time when the Ministry of Immigration had attempted to deport him when his work permit had expired. So, I was open but curious about what I might discover upon meeting with Kantai. We had a long session of over two hours. I did not take notes from our conversation but until today I have vivid memories of both what he said and what was left unsaid, as well as the many questions that arose.

My first and lasting impression was that here was a rather unreliable, untrustworthy and suspicious character. I wondered about the judgment of Kaiser in trusting this young man. I however did not quickly share my views with my confreres until I had time to digest and reflect on what he had told me.

In the meantime, I discovered that Kantai had visited the late Njuguna Mutahi of Kenya Human Rights Commission (KHRC) on the nearby Gatanga Road and also made contact with Kivutha Kibwana – currently Governor of Makueni and then spokesman for the National Convention Executive Council (NCEC). This appeared rather strange behaviour for a man in hiding who claimed his life was in danger. Fortunately, I knew both so we were quickly able to exchange notes and strategise together.

What disturbed me most about Kantai was that he appeared like a compulsive liar. He contradicted himself often when questioned in depth about his earlier utterances. He also claimed that he was brought to State House Mombasa by Sunkuli and offered 10 million Kenyan Shillings by President Moi to betray Kaiser. He claimed that he refused, but never shared the information with Kaiser even though they lived at different ends of the same parish house in Lolgorian. Whether Kantai was just psychotic, unstable or unreliable it mattered not, I just felt that Kaiser should not have depended on this young man to the extent that it appeared he had. I was also very disturbed that he was sharing the same compound with me in Nairobi even if it was only for a very brief period.

What made me most nervous about the catechist, however, was that when asked where he thought was the safest place for him to reside, he quickly replied Kitale – my then place of residence. Call it instinct or my guardian angel or both, but my body has always warned me when personal danger was near and I have always listened to its promptings. I could be forgiven for thinking that I was the next target if he were to seek refuge in Kitale town.

After just ten minutes of the two-hour interview with Kantai the warning bells rang that this man is dangerous and must quickly be sent on his way. The Society leadership team in Nairobi had reservations about him also if not quite as serious as my own. After two days, we gave him some cash and assisted him to travel to Tanzania where he stayed for a few months before returning to his home in Lolgorian.

After public demands for a thorough investigation into Kaiser's death, Daniel arap Moi requested the FBI to investigate his death. From the outset it became obvious that they had a predetermined cause of death, and that was suicide. The chief political advisor of the US Embassy came to Kitale in early October and in the presence of Bishop Maurice Crowley and me stated that on the basis of the evidence that they had received they were concluding that Fr Kaiser had committed suicide. I congratulated him saying that he was the only person in Kenya who subscribed to that theory and politely requested that I might leave the room.

Pretty quickly it became obvious that the FBI were determined to propagate the suicide theory even before concluding their investigations and prior to the release of their so-called findings. To debunk and anticipate this I issued an open letter to US Ambassador John Carson as a press release[44] in an attempt to embarrass them into doing a more thorough and honest investigation. It was only the then People Daily that covered the story in depth but they gave it a front-page headline on Kenyatta Day October 20 2000 that read: 'Priest claims FBI will betray Kaiser'.

The American Embassy was obliged to respond and the best they could do was to claim that I was a well-known scaremonger and should be ignored. However, it did delay the report and it was after Easter 2001 before they announced, just as I had forewarned, that Fr Kaiser had committed suicide. Yet most extraordinary of all was the fact that the FBI never signed off on their own report.

It was never very clear why the FBI sleuths facilitated a cover up but the perceived wisdom was that the Americans at that moment needed the cooperation and support of Mr Moi to arrest and extradite the principal suspects in the American Embassy bombing of August 16, 1998 that killed 213 people. Anything that might have frustrated or jeopardised that process would have caused outrage among the American people who were demanding justice for all the victims. It appeared a classic *quid pro quo.*

In any case the Church, his family and the Kenyan public boycotted the release of the report and dismissed it as a sham. They furthermore demanded a public inquest and this was soon granted after Mwai Kibaki replaced Moi in early 2003. I had not come into contact with Kantai again until the inquest began in Naivasha Law Court in August 2003. For two days I attended with Sr Nuala, Fr William Klaver of the Mill Hill Missionaries, and the family lawyer on the case, Mr Mbuthi Gethinji. On those two days Kantai testified. He was a nervous witness, much more uneasy than in my previous encounters, as he clutched his rosary beads every time he was asked difficult questions in the cross-examination.

Mr Gethinji was unhappy with the evidence. He requested the court to detain Kantai's passport until such time as the inquest was complete and the conclusions made public. The court declined. Kantai left the country the next day and flew to Lusaka where he remained until such time as he was granted a visa to the USA. His desire to travel to the land of opportunity was with the intention to marry a lady called Camille, a blood relative of Kaiser, whom he met when she first visited Lolgorian a few years previously. The story seems incredible, right out of an Agatha

---

44   https://allafrica.com/stories/200010200082.html

Christie thriller. As they say, reality is frequently more unbelievable than fiction. There they live until today.

The inquest was later transferred to the Nairobi courts with Chief Magistrate Maureen Odera now assigned to hear it. One hundred and eleven witnesses in all testified. The FBI were also invited and given an opportunity to present their evidence. They were given three different dates to attend but they neither responded nor sent any written testimony. Of course, that spoke volumes about the credibility and seriousness of their so-called investigations. The inquest concluded in July 2007 and on 1 August Chief Magistrate Maureen Odera read her judgement. She ruled out the suicide theory but stated that on the basis of evidence presented before the court she could not identify who the killers were. Nevertheless, she named several individuals including Kantai, game wardens and Julius Sunkuli who should be investigated further.

In her ruling[45] she referred to Kantai in these words: *'His evidence was in the court's view unreliable, evasive and contradictory'.*[46] *She proceeded to refer to him in these words, 'The duplicity of this witness is clearly evident by the fact that despite his having been a close confidant of the late Fr Kaiser he used his closeness to get information on the location of the two girls at the FIDA safe house. He then led police and a group of councillors to the house from where the girls were "rescued".*[47]

She furthermore remarked that by his own admission in court Kantai was involved in acts of arson against clash victims. She questions, *'why such a witness who admitted to both perjury and arson in open court was allowed to leave the stand (In Naivasha). No attempt was made to arrest and charge him for offences which by his own admission he committed'.*[48]

In summing up his evidence she bluntly states, *'He (Kantai) is one person who in the court's view needs to be interrogated further to establish what role if any he may have played in the death of Fr Kaiser'.*[49] *She furthermore states, 'No mean-*

---

45   Inquest Case No 13 of 2003 in The Chief Magistrates Court of Nairobi
46   Op Cit Page 61
47   Op Cit Page 62
48   Op Cit Page 63
49   Op Cit Page 63

ingful investigations into this matter were carried out by Kenyan investigators'.[50]

To date no other investigations have taken place. Interestingly, Maureen Odera is the daughter of the late Tom Mboya, the Kenyan politician who himself was assassinated in July 1969. She is currently a High Court Judge in the Kenyan Judiciary.[51] The likelihood of the killers ever being held accountable for his brutal death is remote at best. However, Kaiser remains a household name for millions in Kenya and a hero for the downtrodden and human rights defenders. As for Kantai he is still living in USA. However, he is not exactly silent as I discovered in 2018.[52]

In August of that year, I visited my family in New York State while recuperating from knee replacement surgery. I also took the opportunity to catch up with Fr William Klaver, earlier mentioned as the Mill Hill priest who tried his level best to get justice for Fr Kaiser. We had not met for almost five years so I made contact with him as he was then serving in a parish in the Bronx area of New York City. Our friendship had its roots in the Kaiser case. We arranged to meet in Grand Central Station on August 24.

I woke early to catch the train to the city and over breakfast perused my emails. To my utter shock and surprise, there was an email out of the blue from Francis Kantai. This was eerie, a very strange feeling that the man I had no contact from for over a decade should write to me on the very day that I was meeting Fr William after five years. This could hardly be mere coincidence. Synchronicity? Something strange was happening between us on that fateful day.

Over lunch I immediately asked William if he had recent contact with Kantai. He replied that he had not heard of him for more than five years. He was completely dumbfounded when I shared with him the email that I received just two hours previously. Incredible, not merely a coincidence! Only a very disturbed and haunted individual could write an email that started with the words, 'I am innocent'. Why did he need to insist on his innocence and why on this of all days after nearly twenty years?

He suggested that I had written in my regular columns in the *Daily Nation* that

---

50 Op Cit Page 68

51 http://johnkaiser.blogspot.com/2010/09/kenyans-can-no-longer-tolerate-impunity.html

52 https://www.nation.co.ke/oped/opinion/father-kaiser-death-just-one-of-many-that-remain-unsolved/440808-3359130-lwe9amz/index.html

he was responsible for the death of Kaiser. Of course, this was another untruth because even if I dared to make such an accusation in a national newspaper it would not have gotten beyond the editor's desk due to the fear of litigation and defamation. The only mention I had made of Kantai was in the context of reporting what the magistrate had recommended, that he should be one of the people who should be further investigated as mentioned above.

Kantai went on to insist that he was convinced that the priest had committed suicide. The only evidence to support that allegation was that he had once found him watching a movie about a priest who committed suicide. Bizarre at best! He also regretted that he had called his son after the priest, Kaiser. Needless to say, I did not respond to his email nor engage him ever thereafter. However, it did confirm my earlier assertions and fears about him being an unreliable and disturbed individual.

Despite not having known Fr Kaiser, he has played a huge part in my personal history and experiences for over twenty years. I cannot even attempt to disentangle myself from his life and death. Maybe I am the medium to finally uncover the truth. There is also of course another connection that brings an obligation with it too. In March 2004, I was awarded the Law Society of Kenya Annual Human Rights Award for my work in Kitale. It is an annual award and it is called the Fr John Anthony Kaiser Award. I was honoured and humbled but also challenged to continue his great work on behalf of the poor and downtrodden. The struggle for truth and justice never ends.

Receiving the Law Society of Kenya Human Rights Award from Vice President of Kenya, Hon Moody Awori, March 2004

With L to R George Kegoro, Secretary General LSK, Ahmednasir Abudullahi, President of LSK and Sr Nuala Brannigan IBVM at the same event

9

NOWHERE TO CALL HOME

✥

What is more sacred or important than having a place that you can call home? Can any nation claim to be developed when its citizens sleep in streets, bus parks and railway stations? How can a family plan for its future when it is continuously threatened with eviction? Yet this is the shocking reality of life for millions of people across the globe.

Worse still the homeless and the evicted are frequently blamed for their own predicament. Instead of criminalising poverty, the poor are criminalised, stigmatised and deemed a burden and a threat to the welfare of society. In Kenya as in many other countries, being poor is almost a crime while mega looters are feted and emulated.

It is estimated that there are 150 million homeless people in the world and 1.6billion people or 20% of the world's population with inadequate housing.[53] In Nairobi 40% or 1.5 million of the population live in informal settlements. In Mombasa the figure is 55% or 600,000.[54] Thousands more live in similar precarious situations all over the country even in rural areas. Their plight is miserable and ought to be a priority for any government or organisation committed to justice and the eradication of poverty.

The Irish are all too familiar with evictions and landlessness having experienced it under the Crown for a century or more, much like the Kenyan experience of the early twentieth century. Some of my own earliest childhood memories are of forced relocation. My father worked as a farm labourer on a farm owned by a settler family in Ireland. Our home was very basic lacking electricity and running water and with a thatched roof. But it was comfortable and it was our home.

However, when the landlord decided to sell the farm, we were not in a position to purchase it or remain on and so were obliged to move out and look for rental accommodation. This search for another home took several months due to a dis-

---

53   https://yaleglobal.yale.edu/content/cities-grow-so-do-numbers-homeless
54   2019 Census

criminatory public housing policy that favoured the ruling elite in Northern Ireland. This was a heart-breaking experience for all our family. It still pains almost sixty years later. Of course, pain can also become life-giving and increase our empathy and compassion for those in similar situations. Providence has allowed that terrible incident to inspire me to respond with compassion and care for the thousands who face demolition and eviction on a daily basis all over Kenya.

In 2002, we received a delegation of very old and impoverished people at our Kitale office. They had lived for more than half a century between the railway line and the Kitale-Eldoret highway in an area which is mostly in Lugari constituency in Kakamega County. Anyone who has ever passed this main road would be familiar with their plight of abject poverty. They had just been given 30 days' notice to vacate by Kenya Railways Corporation. They needed support and we immediately directed our advocate Jeremiah Samba to file a case in the High Court to prevent their abrupt eviction.

The case was heard in Bungoma High Court and a lorry load of the affected families filled the court for the hearing. The judge was moved by their presence and insisted that more benches should be provided in the crowded court to ensure that the complainants did not have to sit on the floor. Of course, their decision to attend and be recognised did have an effect on the court as the judiciary too has a human face behind the gowns and legal procedures.

The judge gave a favourable ruling, stating that if people had stayed there for half a century without interference or threats, they could not be evicted without Kenya Railways providing alternative land for occupancy.[55] He also ruled that the quit notice was unprocedural and illegal. The claimants were granted temporary orders until such time as Kenya Railways met the court obligations. Sixteen years later they are still on the land even if their situation is quite desperate and deserving of humanitarian assistance.

A similar scenario unfolded in the informal settlement of Kibera in Nairobi in early 2004. Kenya Railways once more were the accused party as they gave notice to 60,000 residents to vacate their property within thirty metres of either side of the railway line. Such forced eviction was both illegal and immoral I argued in a series of Op-Eds submitted to the national press.[56]

---

55   Forced Evictions – Towards Solutions: UN Habitat Page 24
56   Sunday Nation, Talking Point February 29th 2004

The major campaign work on this imminent eviction was done by the CJPC of Christ the King Parish in Kibera who lived right among the affected communities. In a clever and highly publicised move they roped the Papal Nuncio (the Pope's diplomatic representative in Kenya) into their cause. Archbishop Giovanni Tonucci happened to be hosting Cardinal Renato Martino from the Vatican at the time. The two eminent gentlemen walked into Kibera along the railway line and made a passionate appeal to President Mwai Kibaki in front of local and international press to call off the threatened eviction.

The tactic worked and the masses were given reprieve at least for the time being. I was once again moved by the kind gesture of Archbishop Tonucci to write in appreciation of my efforts to highlight the matter in the national press adding that Cardinal Martino too had acknowledged the same before returning to Rome. Small and large victories should be noted and celebrated as they are few and far between.

Kibera of course is the very public face of hardship and suffering as an informal settlement because it is located between Langata Road and the southern bypass near the centre of Nairobi. It is not as hidden from the public view as other slums like Mukuru or Korogocho. Due to its visibility and renown, there are opportunities for advocacy and human rights that should not be passed over. The Christ the King Team in Kibera then invited me to join them on a permanent basis since we had already worked in partnership and one of the priests who worked there, Peter Finegan, was a member of the same religious congregation as myself.

The scheduled transfer was to take place in January 2006. However, I was informed the previous November that Archbishop Ndingi wanted to see me in his office at Holy Family Basilica. Once again, I had uneasy feelings about the pending meeting and when Ndingi finally addressed the matter my worst fears were confirmed. In a sentence that I recall with ease he said that he could not allow me to come to Nairobi because with Raila Odinga and myself in Kibera the place would surely burn! I was stuck for words upon hearing that utterance.

There was an opportunity to respond which I availed of but the archbishop had clearly made up his mind. There was going to be no reversal of the decision so I politely requested to leave and the conversation ended there. The decision was heart-breaking but not entirely surprising. There were already very many voices within and outside the Church that were very uncomfortable with the idea that I would find space to operate within the nation's capital. The archbishop's decision made life a lot easier for them.

In a bit of a dilemma as to what to do next, I resolved that it was time to take a break from the front line and update myself on what was happening globally. I enrolled for a one-year LLM in International Human Rights Law in Belfast and began studies in early September 2006. I also took the opportunity to spend more quality time with my family in Ireland. In January of the following year the Institute of Social Ministry at Tangaza College in Nairobi offered me an opportunity to join their team on completion of my studies. However, Bishop Ndingi once again intervened and categorically stated that I was not welcome in Nairobi, despite the fact that Tangaza was a college independent of the Catholic Archdiocese of Nairobi.

Yet when one door is closed God does frequently manage to open another. The invitation to work in Mombasa came from the late Archbishop Boniface Lele. This was a new venture for my congregation as we had not previously ministered at the coast. After a quick visit I agreed to give it a try providing that we could establish the first parish in Mombasa based in an informal or people's settlement. That was how I arrived in Bangladesh and Kibarani in Mombasa West.

Arriving in October 2007, the challenge of immersing ourselves in the heart of a community struggling to eke out a living was immense. It took several months of negotiations to conclude an agreement with the structure owners to give us a space to construct a building that would give us a presence in the community. In the end we acquired one third of an acre and in the first five years built a church, nursery school, dispensary, community hall and a home. Up until today the church doesn't have a title deed and the threat of eviction, while reduced, is still real.

By late 2008 the need to give space and a forum to represent the local people gave rise to the birth of Haki Yetu Organisation. Haki Yetu ('Our Rights' in Kiswahili) was the slogan used by the supporters of the ODM Party led by Raila Odinga who insisted that the general election of 2007 was stolen. The protests were national and indeed the epicentre of the Mombasa violence was in Bangladesh where the roads were closed for two days in street protests as the neighbouring estate of Mikindani was raided and shops and bars looted. However, despite the negative connotations that may have been associated with the name, we felt that it best represented the aspirations and hopes that we had for our organisation. It was a bold and defiant gesture but we would not apologise for that.

Haki Yetu operated under the shade of a tree for six months and its total posses-sions were contained in a single metal box. When the box was open, the office was functioning. But despite its humble beginnings it slowly made an impact thanks to the tireless efforts of local mobiliser John Paul Obonyo and lawyer Carolyne Ikanda. The two built strong and vibrant networks and began engaging with other like-minded organisations in the Coast. However, the threat of eviction was never far away.

In September 2010, a director of a law firm informed me that he had been told by a senior manager in Kenya Power and Lighting that they had received instructions to disconnect electric power at midnight to the whole settlement of 20,000 people. Thereafter the national government would send in the bulldozers and with the su-pervision of the police demolish all the structures in the entire settlement. It was a distressing moment as I did not want to overreact, but I could not ignore the likeli-hood of the imminent demolitions.

After informing and mobilising the entire community I called the Minister for Lands, Mr James Orengo, and informed him of the threats. He promised to halt the demo-litions but the community remained vigilant, ready to resist any invasion or eviction. Nobody slept that night; police arrived but prudently stayed outside the settlement. The local MP, Ramadhan Kajembe, arrived late in the night but his vehicle was pelted with stones, as there was little love from the community for their elected representative. The threat passed and a few days later Orengo arrived on the ground to reassure the community that as long as he retained the lands docket in the power sharing government they should not worry about any evictions.

That was a huge relief and as the Church continued its building programme many were encouraged to do small but very important home improvements to their own houses. The ripple effect of courage and positive thinking was making a difference. Kibarani however was another challenge altogether. Most of its several thousand residents survived on the pickings of the local dumpsite that was notorious all over Kenya. It was also infamous for harbouring most of the city's criminal element.

Like Bangladesh the area was always under threat from so called private develop-ers. There was one major difference between the two places as regards the issue of land ownership and that was that while most of the land in Bangladesh was government owned, the land in Kibarani was entirely in the hands of tycoons who had acquired title through their friendships with Daniel arap Moi. As a result, the latter were much more likely to press their case and to use their illegally acquired land for personal and business gain; maybe even to sell it. It was much easier to resist and challenge the anonymous government who would soon get tired if there was enough resistance from the communities.

Those who lived in Kibarani were much more vulnerable and this proved to be the case when evictions took place in April 2012. Yet the genesis of the problem was much earlier. In what appeared as providence at work once more, I was perusing the advertising section of the *Daily Nation* when I spotted a notice from Momba-sa High Court giving the respondents 30 days to inform the court as to why they should not be evicted for occupying land in Kibarani that they did not own. It is extraordinary that courts up until today allow notices and orders to be served on the poor through newspapers while there was not a single person named in the same suit who could afford to buy or read the newspaper. John Paul immediately took the court service to our advocate, Jengo, and a response was served on all the named parties within the stipulated thirty days.

However, this did not guarantee protection for the community as on a wet Saturday morning three bulldozers, forty police and a gang of hired goons descended on the community and began unmercifully demolishing homes. We tried calling everyone of importance to stop the destruction but to no avail. Crowds came to watch but the gangs armed with crude weapons together with the riot police kept all of us at bay. All we could do was take photos and video footage of the damage. It was a painful experience supervised by the court bailiff who had acquired illegal court orders by way of deception. The hired youth left the scene of their dirty crimes on police vehi-cles; but not before we captured photos of them that we would use later in litigation.

The destruction continued for several hours and the heavy machinery returned for a second day but this time they were repulsed by the youth in the community with reinforcements from Bangladesh. On the following Monday we returned to court to stop any further demolitions or development on the land since the matter had previously been filed and was awaiting a hearing date. Jengo and Company Advocates then filed a civil case against the bailiff, the company claiming land ownership and the police for all being party to an illegal eviction. To date the case is still proceeding in Mombasa High Court as are three more related cases on the other plots of land in Kibarani.

Courts are a last resort for communities under threat from eviction as rulings are frequently very conservative and cautious giving priority to the sanctity of title over the needs and livelihoods of the at-risk communities. Besides, most courts do not bother to inquire as to how one acquired title, whether the process was legal or not, or even to check whether the title itself is genuine. However, when Dr Willy Mutunga was Chief Justice (2011-16) he gave the judiciary an image which was more just and sympathetic to the poor and this was often reflected in the appointment of judges who produced jurisprudence that was in line with the principles and values of the 2010 Constitution.

Willy, as he was popularly known, was out of the country when the Kibarani eviction took place. He did, however, take my phone call on the day of the evictions. He also promised to come to Mombasa and meet with the people. Prudence determined that he could not enter Kibarani lest he be judged to be interfering with a case that was before court (sub judice). He did come to Bangladesh, however, the following month along with a good half of the Mombasa judiciary.

His presence and solidarity with the people spoke volumes, much more than anything he could add in his address. At last people began to realise and experience what 'Access to Justice' really meant. The visit ended with 80-year-old Lucia - whose home had been demolished in Kibarani - giving the Chief Justice a broom and telling him to sweep the judiciary clean of all corruption. The damage had been done, but his presence and encouraging words gave many hope and energy to rebuild their little homes and start afresh.

They say that justice usually goes to those who can endure the most. If that is the case then the people of Kibarani will most definitely succeed. The current signs are that the other parties claiming ownership of the land are getting tired and no real threats have come to the community in recent years. However, the resolve of the community is particularly due to the efforts of John Paul who has moulded them into a powerful united force, with its own land committee who never fail to turn up in large numbers in court at their own expense.

The people know it is their struggle so they must invest in it themselves. It is their lives and livelihoods that are at stake. They have also resolved that if forcefully evicted from the land again they will walk the fifteen kilometres to the City Mall in Nyali and occupy the buildings that house the most expensive stores in Mombasa, since the owner also has a disputed plot in Kibarani. With nowhere else to go they will tell the tycoon 'we are coming to stay in your home since you have evicted us from ours'. That indeed is a serious threat!

But there are emerging signs of recognition of their right to shelter and services. The area has electricity now, a quality primary school built by the Church and significant investment in structures by the residents themselves.

However, every time I spot a bulldozer moving ominously in the direction of informal settlements, my heart churns and a cold sweat breaks out on my brow. Threats to the existence of the poor are as real today as twenty years ago. There have been no genuine efforts made to regularise land issues in informal settlements and government plans to build cheap housing units have failed miserably. After committing itself to building 500,000 units in five years the current government has completed a mere 2,000 after three years.[57]

The problem is not insurmountable as there are many options that could be replicated or adopted from around the globe. What is missing is a government that has a heart for its citizens, that recognises that the disadvantaged are a hidden treasure who can transform the face of the country if given an opportunity and the dignity and respect that each of them deserves.

That remains the belief, inspiration and the vision of Haki Yetu. It is best captured in the words of Pope Francis, 'I want a Church which is poor and for the poor. We are called to lend our voice to their causes, but also to be their friends, to listen to them, to speak for them and to embrace the mysterious wisdom which God wishes to share with us through them'.[58]

---

57 https://www.theeastafrican.co.ke/news/ea/Only-one-percent-of-kenya-big-four-agenda
     -targets-met-so-far/4552908-5423128-c1kcgrz/index.html
58 Evangelii Gaudium, No 198

Illegal eviction in Kibarani, Mombasa, April 2012

Hired and armed goons transported in a Police Vehicle during the eviction.

Activists disown Joho's Sh200bn housing plan

Civil society groups deny drafting legal agreement to safeguard tenants' rights in planned upgrade

BY GITONGA MARETE

@GitongaMarete

gmarete@ke.nationmedia.com

Members of civil society have rejected a proposal by the Mombasa County Government to participate in drafting a legal agreement for tenants in a planned Sh200 billion housing project.

The county plans to replace old houses in 10 estates — Khadija, Miritini, Changamwe, Tudor, Mzizima, Buxton, Likoni, Nyerere, Tom Mboya and Kaa Chonjo — with new ones in partnership with private developers.

Despite opposition from some tenants and politicians, Governor Hassan Joho insists he will carry on with the project in which sitting tenants are expected to own the houses.

Property developers have started putting in their bids for the development of the estates.

Mr Joho has said civil society groups Kituo Cha Sheria, Juhudi and Linda Africa would help draft the agreements.

However, two of the organisations have denied that they would be part of the agreements, with Juhudi's executive director Simon Katee saying he was not aware of the development.

Under the banner "coast land non-state actors", the organisations said they were not involved.

The groups falling the banner are Actionaid, Muslims for Human Rights (Muhuri), Kenya Land Alliance, Transparency International (Kenya), Haki Yetu, Kenya National Commission on Human Rights, Kituo Cha Sheria, Juhudi and Ujamaa.

Discord

LEADERS, TENANTS ALSO UNHAPPY

The renewal of the housing estates has met stiff resistance from some leaders and occupants.

Wiper leaders Senator Hassan Omar and Nyali MP Hezron Bolo Awiti have questioned the legality of the project, saying the county assembly was used to rubberstamp the project.

The project has also attracted opposition from a businessman, Mr Suleiman Shahbal, who recently joined hands with Khadjia Estate residents fearing displacement.

"The suggestion that we commit ourselves to draft a legal agreement the tenants is far from the truth. request that such reference be refied and that we will not undertake such task," they said in a letter sign by Fr Gabriel Dolan of Haki Yetu a Paul Obonyo, on behalf of the grou secretariat.

"We deliberated extensively on t project and concluded it targets h income earners whose appetite luxury urban apartments is now too familiar," they said.

However, County Lands and Housi Executive Antony Njaramba claim all the other groups had agreed to t plan except Fr Dolan.

"We are aware that some individu are opposed to the project but as far we are concerned, adequate consul tions were done," he said.

Speaking to *Nation* yesterday, Ken Land Alliance Mombasa chapter boa member Shamzan Nagib said the let had been sent with the blessing of the mentioned civil societies.

"We are aware of the letter and su port its contents. We are not opposed the project but to the manner in whi it is being pushed," he said.

"This is public land yet they are n telling us how it will change to priva when the houses are built and sold. V need to thrash out these issues befo the project kicks off," he added.

15/04/16

10

DEVOLVED FUNDS AND BROKEN PROMISES

Devolution was the big selling point in the 2010 Referendum for a new constitution. For half a century, whole regions of Kenya had been deprived of services and infrastructure while other areas received more than their fair share of the national cake. Some counties had never seen a tarred road while others had known nothing else. Inequality had contributed greatly to ethnic conflicts and fuelled belief that some were definitely more equal than others. KANU had continuously favoured areas that were loyal to the executive and shared the same ethnicity as the president. Loyalty brought development; disloyalty brought poverty.

Devolution was expected to be the panacea for all these ills. Not only would the forty-seven counties receive at least 15% of the national budget, but it was presumed that ethnic rivalry would reduce as counties would be able to implement their own development programmes and not feel obliged to compete for the leftovers from the big five tribes. It was also presumed that devolved governance would reduce the conflict over the presidential elections that had produced strife and chaos every five years. No longer would the contest be a winner-takes-all as the voters in the counties could also elect their own county assembly. In other words, if your party candidate did not take the presidential seat there was always the chance to have your say about how your county would be governed and how it might progress.

That was the theory, so what about the practice? Truth be told, devolved governance has had a significant impact in Kenya. In particular the regions that were most deprived and neglected have made considerable progress in the provision of medical services, roads and town development. From Wajir to Turkana, from Tana River to Marsabit, Kenyans are experiencing services in the past few years that they had only viewed from afar for the first half century of independence. Hospitals are better equipped and staffed, schools are being constructed and local economies are thriving in a manner not experienced before. Of course, corruption too has evolved and been devolved but, as one cynic suggested, at least the money is being stolen locally and not in Nairobi so it trickles down to the local economy at the county level. That too cannot be disputed.

There is much less satisfaction, however, with the performance of the devolved institutions in the large urban centres of Mombasa, Nairobi, Kisumu and Nakuru. In part, this is because these municipal authorities were already receiving an unfair share of decentralised disbursements before the advent of devolution. They were also saddled through the new constitution with managing regional hospitals that now served up to six counties in the province. That meant that a huge percentage of their budget was taken up by the health sector which was one of the principal ministries devolved to the counties.

Mombasa is an interesting study in any analysis of devolution. By 2013, when Hassan Ali Joho was elected Governor, he inherited a bankrupt and corrupt municipal authority that provided little or no services to the citizens. Joho took advantage of the mood for change and through a very savvy and slick electronic and social media campaign endeared himself to the public. He presented himself as a new generation of leader, the digital kind, and was branded as a celebrity who donned expensive, youthful fashions. His appeal was strong and his face was everywhere. He even dared to name himself Sultan Joho, without recourse to the fact that such a name carries historically, negative connotations for the indigenous communities in the Coastal Region

However, as they say, on the ground things can be very different. At Haki Yetu we attempted to engage the county executive over many issues that were of particular concern for the poor in the informal settlements namely water, sanitation, land and housing. Along with other strong partners like Kituo cha Sheria, we put particular emphasis on the issue of security of tenure for slum dwellers and the allocation of government land for the provision of schools and medical facilities for the people's settlements.

The county executive for land for most of this time was Francis Thoya, who proved himself a strong support to communities that faced eviction. Solidarity, sympathy and courage were his trademark but he lacked support from the executive, so he ended up behaving like a firefighter rather than an agent of change. Three examples of Joho's broken promises and crazy dreams will illustrate his dismal failure to bring any meaningful change to the neediest of the coastal city's residents.

In 2014, we had identified a two-acre plot along the main Nairobi highway at Bangladesh that would have been very suitable for the construction of a mixed day secondary school, since there was no such facility for the thousands of young people in the area. We were aware that it was government land (Kenya Railways) but it had been lying idle for years. We approached Joho and requested him to acquire the land for us. He appeared very enthusiastic and committed to the project. We arranged for a ground breaking ceremony on his suggestion and he came along with a bevy of media personnel and a lot of fanfare. He told us to proceed and start the project and he would secure the land.

In our naivety we drew up plans and signed a contract with a reputable construction firm who submitted the building plans for approval to the same governor's office. A few months later the contractor started digging foundations to erect a perimeter wall. On the second day of the work, dozens of police came and arrested the workers for trespassing on private property. When Joho was asked to intervene, he made promises and threats but did nothing to secure the land for the proposed school. Six years later Kenya Railways leased the same land to a Somali business-man, but he too has not been able to develop the plot due to resistance from the community who still want the school plan to proceed.

It became rather obvious in 2016 that the Governor was more interested in acquir-ing land than in allocating it, as shown by another incident in Bangladesh. Early in the year, the Governor arrived unexpectedly and after walking through the settle-ment announced that he was building a road that would pass right through the area and connect it to Mikindani estate and link with the undeveloped ocean land. He further stated that no one would be compensated and so they should remove their structures immediately before they were forcefully removed. This was an illegal decree yet he dared to proceed.

The community was astonished since they neither had requested the road nor did they see any benefit to them in its construction. On the contrary, the road would disrupt their businesses, endanger children's lives, evict many families and destroy church buildings that provided educational and medical services to the poor. To-gether with other affected parties Haki Yetu went to court. Our plaint was that there was no public participation, the project was not budgeted for nor requested, and it was illegal and criminal to evict people without compensation or offering them an alternative place to live.

The case was heard by Mombasa High Court as a matter of urgency and it was no surprise to us that the court stopped the project on the grounds that we had argued. Joho was not happy and, in several forums, referred to me as 'an enemy of devel-opment'.[59] Many observers believe that the real aim of the road was to get access

---

59   https://diasporamessenger.com/2016/09/rival-groups-disrupt-joho-speech/

to the beach plots that had not been allocated or developed. It would appear that lucrative land and beach plots were more important to some than the lives, livelihoods and safety of the people of Bangladesh. Yet the road was budgeted for and money allocated for its construction as we later discovered.

In early January 2019 the Mombasa Senator, Mohammed Faki, requested to meet me. In the course of our meeting over a cup of coffee he explained that the Public Accounts Committee (PAC) of parliament was pursuing the funds allocated for the road and he wanted support in defending Joho or even suggestions for an alternative project. It was pretty obvious that Joho was in a fix but I declined to get involved since he had driven roughshod over the community in his dubious plans and should not expect any rescue plan from our side.

Indeed, relationships with the Governor did not improve when his dream project of constructing 30,000 housing units in the city was questioned and legally challenged by Haki Yetu and another organisation, Kituo cha Sheria. The launch of Joho's fancy project was a glitzy affair with glossy brochures, 3D-imaging and dozens of media folk from Kenya and abroad. It looked an attractive and progressive project that would change the face of Kenya's second city. The plan was to demolish the six old estates that comprised of 3,100 units and to construct 30,000 apartments that would range from bedsitters, through one- and two-bedroom apartments to penthouses. It looked like a great move to address the housing shortage in Mombasa but, as they say, all that glitters is not gold.[60]

Initially we began inquiries as to how the project would be financed and whether there were opportunities for renting or ownership especially by those in the informal settlements. The housing minister explained that the total cost of the project would be $2bn (Kshs 200Bn) but that in the Private Public Partnership (PPP) arrangement eighty per cent of the units would go to the investor who would sell them off as follows: bedsitter (Shs 1.5m or $15,000 and a one-bedroom Shs 2.5m; two-bedroom Shs 4m while a three-bedroom would go for between six and nine million shillings. That meant that the county would remain with 6,000 units that could be occupied by the current tenants of the old estates, and some new tenants who would also have the opportunity to buy them outright or on a higher purchase scheme.[61]

60   https://mobile.nation.co.ke/news/politics/Groups-reject-Joho-homes-plan--/3126390-3159870-item-1-aithb7z/index.html

61   https://www.the-star.co.ke/counties/coast/2016-04-04-johos-sh200bn-mombasa-plan-

There was nothing cheap about the new units; the prices quoted were even higher than the market rates. This in our opinion was a project designed to provide housing for the middle class, who were already in a position to acquire a mortgage to own their own home. This project would contribute zero to the provision of low cost, affordable housing for the 60% of the population that lived in the informal settlements.[62] It looked more like real estate investment rather than a response to the housing needs.

Besides, the proposal would allow a private enterprise to take over government land, build housing units and sell them off, without in any way compensating government for the loss of the land. Since there were no provisions as to how the current occupants would be relocated during the construction, nor guarantees that they would become beneficiaries of the new units, they too opposed the plan. Mr Joho was not happy when we filed the case in Mombasa High Court in September 2016 and it was scheduled to be heard the following month. The hope was that the court would address our claims that there was insufficient information and consultation on the project, and also a cloud of secrecy around the tendering and financing.

To our surprise and huge disappointment, the High Court dismissed our case without costs.[63] Judge JP Otieno ruled that there was sufficient information available in the public domain to allow the project to proceed. He did, however, rule that we should be allowed to access all information as the work progressed.[64] This at least allowed us to be recognised as interested parties and stakeholders who had a right to be heard in any further housing development initiative.

We nevertheless appealed the verdict and brought the matter to the Court of Appeal. Again, there was no joy here as our appeal was dismissed in a December 2018 ruling. Both rulings focused on the threshold of public participation. The court in its usual conservative nature set a very low threshold and ignored the fact that at least 90% of those with genuine housing needs knew nothing of what Joho's government was planning. A few news items and glossy brochures in a language that

reeks-of-dictatorship/

62   https://www.standardmedia.co.ke/article/2000196238/opposition-mounts-against-joho-s-sh90-billion-housing-project

63   https://www.nation.co.ke/counties/mombasa/Joho-Sh200bn-housing-project/1954178-3496398-lpvub4z/index.html

64   https://www.capitalfm.co.ke/news/2017/01/joho-accused-sh1bn-garbage-collection-tender-scam/

most did not understand – English – was as much as was done. The court failed to recognise that everyone is a stakeholder when public housing is on the agenda.

We may have lost the battle but not the war. We continued to liaise with the current tenants who went to court and succeeded in convincing another judge that until such time as they were compensated and relocated, they could not be removed from their present homes.[65] Most interesting and baffling of all is that the County Government has not moved forward a single inch in five years in the implementation of the project, despite being given the green light by the courts.

Many suggest that the Governor just came up with this pipedream project to advance his re-election in the 2017 poll. Others surmise that perhaps the aim was to gain possession of the land. Then again there is the possibility that this was a huge scam involving dubious investors and that our continuous involvement in the exercise gave them cold feet. Whatever the case the project stalled and the emphasis was then put on just renovating and repairing one or two of the existing estates in a much scaled-down version.

Yet the housing needs are as pressing as ever, not just in Mombasa, but in the whole of Kenya where President Kenyatta made housing one of the four pillars of his 2017 presidential manifesto. The government speaks mainly of 'affordable housing'. By that they mean a market-based home ownership notion which is beyond the reach of most of the urban population. On the other hand, social justice advocates speak of 'social housing' which is decent rental accommodation at an affordable price for the masses who can never aspire to own their own homes especially in urban areas.

The government planned to build 1million homes by 2022, with 80% being the affordable kind and a mere 200,000 set aside for rental. Currently they have completed a mere 2,000 units. The housing crisis remains but the bigger challenge is the unaddressed land tenure system in urban settlements. If most residents in these areas were guaranteed security of tenure, even under a community title, they themselves would develop their own homes over a period of time. The government role would be to supervise and guide homeowners in their home improvement and perhaps offer soft loans where possible. In that way the citizens themselves would solve the housing shortage.

---

65 https://www.standardmedia.co.ke/article/2001273805/court-of-appeal-stops-tenant-evic tion-in-joho-s-multi-billion-housing-project

Pope Francis puts this quite beautifully in his Encyclical Letter, Laudato Si' as he echoed our own thinking and inspiration on the right to housing, 'In some places, where makeshift shanty towns have sprung up, this will mean developing those neighbourhoods rather than razing or displacing them. When the poor live in unsanitary slums or in dangerous tenements, "in cases where it is necessary to relocate them, in order not to heap suffering upon suffering, adequate information needs to be given beforehand, with choices of decent housing offered, and the people directly involved must be part of the process"'.[66] Regretfully, it would appear that neither Governor Joho nor President Kenyatta have heeded the Pontiff's advice and guidelines on this most basic of human rights.

The Pope visited Washington DC in September 2015 and stated categorically, 'Let me be clear. There is no social or moral justification, no justification whatsoever, for the lack of housing'. Maybe he should have repeated the same message when he came to Nairobi two months later. At Haki Yetu, we continue to expend energy and resources on promoting the need and right to housing while also addressing the land questions. The two issues are inseparable for the world can never address the housing shortage until it tackles head on the land ownership question, especially in the large cities.

In 2020, Joho resurrected his dream housing project. He announced that the first redevelopment would take place at Buxton Estate. This time around there were indeed more public meetings on the subject with the current tenants, the public at large and civil society organisations. It appeared that he was learning from previous mistakes and was acknowledging the importance of proper public participation in any major development project. Again, he assured the residents that they would be given compensation for being displaced and given first preference in occupancy and ownership of the new housing units.

Yet, eighty per cent of the housing units would go to the private developer in the private public partnership. This hardly seems like a win-win situation either for the county or for the residents. The fact that the partnership is also with a company belonging to Suleiman Shabhal a politician who has declared his interest in the gubernatorial seat in Mombasa in the 2022 elections also raises questions about the issue of conflict of interests.

The plan includes mortgage options as well as rentals but there are few details

---

66   Laudato Si No 152 (quoting Compendium of Social Doctrine of the Church 482)

about the conditions under which the banks will enter into agreements on the mortgages. The ground breaking was to take place on January 1st 2021 but nothing has happened to date. Haki Yetu requested the County Executive for Lands and Housing to provide us with all the information regarding tendering, costing, environmental assessment report and many other pertaining matters. However, no information has been provided despite the fact that the earlier court rulings clearly stated that all the information required and requested should be availed. As a result, Haki Yetu filed a case in court in December 2020 demanding that the court order the release of the requested documents.

In the past year, 2020, many complaints have emerged about unfinished projects and wasted resources in the County Government of Mombasa. At Haki Yetu we investigated some of those projects and produced the first in a series of booklets exposing fraud and wastage at the county government. The booklet entitled, "Unfinished Business and Wasted Resources" dealt with a half dozen projects ranging from sports facilities to educational establishments and road developments.

We uncovered huge wastage and over expenditure in the use of public resources. Thirty million shillings ($300,000) had been spent on an Early Childhood Development (ECD) Centre in Chaani yet it has never been completed and thieves have removed the iron sheets and fittings from the buildings. Millions more had been spent on road upgrading but are in a worse state than before. Sports facilities including all weather football pitches were shoddily done and abandoned.

Devolution is not the panacea for all the ills of neglect and bad governance. There have been achievements in the past decade but civil society actors at the local level must be brave enough to confront Governors who are behaving like mini-Presidents and who possess resources to compromise local media and intimidate any voices of dissent. The battle for accountability has now moved to the grassroots and it demands a whole new energy and courage from the public.

Activist and Musician Juliani visits Bangladhesh and gives his voice to illegal evictions, 2015

11

A CHURCH OUT ON THE STREETS

Ever since the first followers of Jesus began responding to his mandate to go out to the whole world and preach the Good News[67] his followers have witnessed to the Gospel message in a variety of ministries. The early Church soon recognised the need to not neglect the poor and widows and created the ministry of diaconate[68] while still continuing the work of evangelisation. Charity and mercy are an integral part of the Gospel message and many thousands down the years have devoted their lives as religious people to care for the sick, feed the hungry and educate the next generation. The Gospel is a call to change oneself and the world but there is rarely agreement among Church officials as to how that change should take place.

In particular there is certain unease within the Church hierarchy about working for justice, challenging oppressive systems and protesting about injustices. Yet Catholic Social Teaching (CST) has consistently defended the weak, the poor and the exploited for over a hundred years. There is a huge body of excellent social analysis and teachings that have influenced world bodies and policy makers as well as Church members over the years. The challenge and the differences come in the attempts to implement this powerful and prophetic social teaching at the grassroots level.

There is a huge gap between the theory in the teaching and putting it into practice, and so the Church is often accused of condemning unjust practices but doing little to alleviate them. The message remains in the pulpit but does not influence the streets. That is why Catholic Social Teaching is often referred to as the Church's best kept secret.

But one is obliged to ask, in whose interest is it that the church keeps CST secretive and away from the masses? Is the social teaching so radical and dangerous that it is risky to let the faithful get it into their own hands? Is the Church itself afraid that it may be under scrutiny if the social teachings are made available to the public? If the Church had had a more open, accountable and democratic structure for

---

67   Mark 16:15
68   Acts 6:1-6

engagement with the public, would the evils of sexual abuse not have been avoided and the lives of thousands of children been better protected? Does the Church want public institutions to be accountable but still remain itself as an institution that is accountable only to God? Those questions remain as a challenge both for theologians and practitioners.

The Church is indeed mandated to carry out the work of God yet it is also a human institution, with its own limitations, weaknesses and structures. Having such a huge global network is, of course, a huge advantage in terms of messaging and mobilisation. But when that same body is hierarchically structured and dominated by men it is very difficult to get consensus in acting for change although the teaching on justice is not at all ambivalent.

Fifty years ago the Synod of Bishops meeting in Rome produced a document entitled, 'Justice in the World' that clearly stated, 'Christian love of neighbour and justice cannot be separated", and "Action on behalf of justice and participation in the transformation of the world fully appear to us as a constitutive dimension of the preaching of the Gospel, or, in other words, of the Church's mission for the redemption of the human race and its liberation from every oppressive situation"[69] Justice work is then not an added extra or a fashionable afterthought but a CONSTITUENT element of the Gospel.

This was most clearly understood by the leadership of the Church in Latin America who promoted liberation theology in a way that unapologetically presented a defence of their justice ministry by referring to it as an, 'Option for the Poor'. Liberation Theology went hand in hand with the development of small, neighbourhood, Christian communities who met weekly to reflect on the Gospel as an inspiration and guide in their lives. The Gospel was alive, relevant and speaking to them in their current situation while calling them to take communal action to address injustices and oppression in their everyday situation.

That of course meant that local communities would now begin to act, question and confront and that is where they ran into difficulties with both civil and Church authorities. Liberation theology then became a threat to many because the Church hierarchy could no longer maintain its cosy relationships with state authorities while its followers were confronting it. Power had been given to the people and the hierarchy was uncomfortable about where that might lead. The Church may have been

---

69   Justice in the World, Paragraphs 34 & 6, Synod of Bishops 1971

happy to negotiate incremental reform in society but the masses who had tasted liberation would not be satisfied with anything but real, substantial change.

Briefly, the term 'Option for the Poor' meant that the Church's mandate included the mission to defend the poor, weak, oppressed and dispossessed and take their side. It also demanded that the poor be not only heard but that they acquire their own platforms to articulate their issues. This did not necessarily mean that the Church would neglect the spiritual welfare of those who were not poor. Rather the call went to them too to play their part in creating a more just and equal society. In practice that meant that the Church too would be under scrutiny and be liable to attack from political regimes. Oscar Romero, (a bishop in El Salvador, assassinated in 1980 and canonised in 2018) summed this position up when he said, 'A Church that does not suffer persecution, but in fact enjoys the privileges and support of the world, is a church which should be afraid because it is not in fact the Church of Jesus Christ'.[70]

Romero realised that opting for the poor came with a price: loss of privilege, status, income and in his case life too. Things were definitely turned upside down by siding with the poor. Yet liberation theology did not take root in Africa in the same manner as it did in Latin America, despite the endemic corruption and massive inequality where hundreds of millions were living below the poverty line. Why one may well ask? Where is the prophetic Christianity evident in Kenyan society today?

Churches concentrated on widespread civic education rather than mobilisation for more radical change. Of course, the fear was that protest would lead to violence and widespread unrest. So, it was left to a few courageous Church leaders to confront and challenge the state and its institutions on behalf of the general public. In effect that worked to some degree but it delayed more meaningful and institutional change for several decades. It also never addressed the widespread poverty and inequality that has made Kenya one of the most socially unequal countries in the world. It did not really facilitate the masses in their own liberation. Instead, the hierarchy spoke and negotiated on their behalf.

 According to Oxfam International, a mere 8,300 Kenyans own 99% of the wealth in the country. Nearly one million children of school-going age are out of school and the government spends a mere 7% of the annual budget on healthcare.[71] All is not

70   Minding the Spirit: The Study of Christian Spirituality, Ed Elizabeth Dryer p 238

71   https://www.oxfam.org/en/kenya-extreme-inequality-numbers December 2017

well as the recently retired Auditor General, Edward Ouko, consistently cited that one third of the national budget is looted each year, and compiled figures suggest that it is as much as 1 trillion Kenya Shillings ($10 billion) per annum.[72] What is the response of the Church to such endemic pilfering of the public coffers?

The twice-yearly pastoral letters from the Bishops give analysis and guidance on governance issues but they do not make an impact. They rarely grab the headlines and certainly do not reach the masses. Pastoral letters appear like a chore that have to be repeated but which lack conviction and support even among the members of the Bishops' Conference itself. A recent campaign on fighting corruption has gained support but it needs more energy, investment and originality to grab the attention of a public who still believe that corruption is a culture that is here to stay and the situation is irreversible. The current emphasis is more on the call for the individual to change rather than on confronting the impunity that is at the root of corruption.

In a culture where corruption is so prevalent it is inevitable then that the Church too will be tainted and tarnished. For the last ten years, politicians have been donating millions of shillings each week to Catholic churches and institutions in Kenya. Most of these 'generous' men – always men – have never explained the source of their massive wealth yet they have been linked to mega corruption scandals and land grabbing as well as the looting of the public coffers for decades.

In my weekly newspaper columns, I have frequently condemned this practice while naming the politicians together with the Bishops who are all too willing to give them a special blessing and a microphone in the sanctuary to criticise their opponents.[73] In the public eye, these millions buy the silence of the Church and prelates become collaborators in crime as a result.[74] No wonder that the header of my Op-Ed column of March 31, 2012 was 'Priests have become commodities for hire'.[75]

The annual prayer breakfast organised by parliament and religious leaders is an exercise in hypocrisy as the same invited guests loot the country, promote a pros-

---

72   https://www.standardmedia.co.ke/business/article/2001305596/the-shame-of-sh1-trillion-queried-yearly-by-auditor

73   Politicians now hijacking God's houses – Saturday Nation, February 4, 2012

74   Politicians paying Church to remain silent, Saturday Nation, October 18, 2014

75   https://www.nation.co.ke/oped/opinion/Priests-have-become-commodities-for-hire-/440808-1376832-nruag2/index.html Saturday March 31, 2012

perity gospel and feast at the expense of the poor.[76] One is often inclined to think that the Church is more inclined to live with the problems of the country rather than feel the obligation and calling to solve Kenya's problems. As a service provider the Church still gives amazing service and witness but is reluctant to ask the hard questions as to how long they must provide basic necessities of food, health care and education while Kenyans are paying billions in taxes to a government that does not serve them.

As a result, Christianity has become an integral and vital part of a dysfunctional society. As part of this arrangement the Church is used to induce, tolerate, and ultimately benefit from, the widespread culture of impunity at all levels of society. There is a very cosy relationship between the religious and political elites in Kenya. They accommodate each other very well.

Of course, there is also the fear factor not only for the individual's security but for his reputation. When an outspoken cleric consistently irritates the ruling class the National Intelligence Service (NIS) can always be called upon to reveal the skeletons hidden in the ecclesiastical cupboards. One friend calls this the 'Ncube Factor' after the very outspoken Archbishop of Bulawayo Pius Ncube who was secretly filmed in a 'compromising position' with a lady friend in 2007. That marked the fall from grace of the outspoken champion of social justice and resulted in the taming of religious leaders all over the continent. That threat most certainly features in the Kenyan Church, even if it is rarely admitted.

Responses by the hierarchy to my writings have been quite ambiguous. When the content exposes the rot in government institutions the reaction can be favourable. However, when a topic touches on the hierarchy or Church teaching it often results in the belt of an episcopal crozier. The local Church does not tolerate any dissent or rocking of the boat from within, as many have discovered over the years.

In July 2012 my Op-Ed Column was entitled 'Church Stand on Family Planning Outdated'.[77] I argued that humanity seemed to have already fulfilled the Creator's command to fill the earth. The Kenyan population was 8 million at independence but had reached 47 million then. There was a real need then for the Church to revisit its objection to 'artificial' family planning methods (contraceptives) since most

---

76   https://www.nation.co.ke/oped/opinion/Would-our-annual-prayers-impress-
      Christ/440808-1920256-10s5p6m/index.html July 20, 2013 Saturday Nation

77   https://www.nation.co.ke/oped/Opinion/Church-stand-on-family-planning-outdated-
      /440808-1459448-powpd8z/index.html July 21, 2012

of the faithful had already rejected 'natural' family planning as unworkable in their families.

This did not go down well with the hierarchy and Cardinal Njue wrote to his fellow Bishops saying that, 'It is not acceptable that an individual should go against the teaching .... on family planning.... and remains to pastor the flock of Christ in any Catholic Church'. That appeared like a threat of excommunication or silencing but I was not going to backtrack or apologise. It most certainly was not an affirmation of the right to freedom of conscience on matters that were not deemed infallible in the Church teaching. Anyhow, I lay low for a short while and weathered the storm but felt affirmed when Pope Francis mentioned in 2015 that responsible parenthood meant that Catholics should not breed like rabbits.[78]

But a further controversy arose around the issue of the neonatal anti-tetanus vaccination programme being rolled out in sixteen districts in March 2014. Women were the target population in the door-to-door campaign since immunity to tetanus can be passed on from mother to infant at childbirth, protecting children who might otherwise develop tetanus shortly after birth. This had caused 555 such deaths in Kenya the previous year. However, the Health Commission of the Bishops Conference claimed that the vaccine was laced with an infertility drug that had left women permanently infertile in other countries. The Bishops Conference supported that stand and bought space in the national press a few days later to explain their position. That spread fear among the population about the legitimacy of the vaccination exercise and many women chose not to get vaccinated as a result.

In my column on the topic, 'Bishops Wrong on Anti-Tetanus Drive' I argued that the Bishops had a moral duty to produce genuine scientific evidence that the vaccine was intended to make Kenyan women barren. It was imprudent and dangerous to cause alarm without scientific evidence and in the process threaten the lives of two million women who were targeted in this exercise.[79] This did not go down well with the Apostolic Administrator of Mombasa, Bishop Emanuel Barbara, who advised me in writing: '*stop communicating your divergent views through the media regarding issues where the position of the Catholic Church has been made known to the public...your behaviour is not creating unity in the Church*'.

---

78 https://www.ncronline.org/news/vatican/dont-breed-rabbits-was-pope-francis-breaking-new-ground-birth-control

79 https://www.nation.co.ke/oped/opinion/440808-2270934-2qmhhd/index.html April 5, 2014

The implicit warning here is that one must support the position of the bishops on a matter critical to the health of the nation's mothers even when there is no scientific evidence to back up that stance. Unity appeared more important than truth and I responded in writing to the good prelate saying that I was willing to publicly alter my position and apologise if proof of their allegations was provided. However, the matter did not end there as in the next round of the campaign in November of the same year, Cardinal Njue once more waded into the debate claiming that the Ministry of Health was: *'incapable and unwilling to stop the permanent poisoning of women'.*[80]

The conflict with the Ministry of Health came to the surface again in June 2016 when the campaign to vaccinate 19 million Kenyans against measles was launched. Once more the Health Commission of the Bishops Conference stated that they 'opposed mass vaccination campaigns until such time as the safety of the vaccinations can be ascertained'.[81] Most Kenyans ignored the Bishops' warning and the campaign met its targets. One wonders will the Church also advise against mass vaccination when the vaccines for Covid-19 become widely available, hopefully this year.

In 2015, however, tests were conducted by independent sources on the anti-tetanus vaccine. Fifty vials presented by the Ministry of Health were closed and declared safe according to the laboratory results. Three presented by the Church had been opened and contaminated. There was no explanation as to who opened the vials or why and how they had been contaminated. There appeared to be mischief in the Church's position. The debate continues but the Church has never produced a single iota of evidence of any vaccine being laced with a hormone that left women permanently infertile. There are also no signs of widespread infertility in the country or any obvious drop in the population growth. No apology to women has been proffered either.

Yet, despite the obvious dilemma of being a priest and a commentator in the secular press, there is enough widespread support for advocacy work through the written word that one does not get discouraged or worried by the occasional hierarchical objection or threat. A huge boost to a more open, humble, simple Church devoted to the poor, however, has been the pontificate of Pope Francis who was

---

80   https://www.nation.co.ke/oped/opinion/Time-to-put-the-tetanus-row-to-rest/440808-2522928-15idr7yz/index.html

81   https://www.nation.co.ke/oped/opinion/Vaccination-saga-continues-to-confuse/440808-3231532-format-xhtml-enrpdlz/index.html June 3, 2016

elected by the conclave of Cardinals in March 2013, after the retirement of Pope Benedict XVI.

In his Encyclical *The Joy of the Gospel (Evangelii Gaudium)* Francis says, '*the Church must not become a useless structure out of touch with people or a self-absorbed cluster made up of a chosen few.*'[82] He goes on to explain what type of Church he prefers, '*I prefer a Church which is bruised, hurting and dirty because it has been on the streets, rather than a Church which is unhealthy from being confined and clinging to its own security...within rules that make us harsh judges, within habits that make us safe, while at our door people are starving and Jesus does no tire of saying to us: "Give them something to eat".*' (Mark 6:37)[83]

Francis said '*the Church cannot and must not remain on the side-lines in the fight for justice*'[84] but his most audacious and incisive words are reserved for occasions when he meets particular groups in the Vatican. One such meeting was in October 2014 when he addressed participants at the World Meeting of Popular Movements. His language was earthy, warm and passionate when he told them, '*One senses that the poor are no longer waiting. You want to be protagonists. You have your feet in the mud. You carry the smell of your neighbourhood, your people, your struggle. We want your voices to be heard – voices that are rarely heard. No doubt this is because your voices cause embarrassment, no doubt it is because your cries are bothersome, no doubt because people are afraid of the change that you seek*'.

This is radical, straight talk never heard from a Pope before and he goes on to challenge governments, agencies and NGOs when he says, '*The scandal of poverty cannot be addressed by promoting strategies of containment that only tranquilize the poor and render them tame and inoffensive*'. Those are the exact words he spoke, not paraphrased or given a fashionable spin. As a rejoinder to those who think this is dangerous talk: '*Some say the Pope is a communist. They do not understand that love for the poor is at the centre of the Gospel. Land, housing and work are sacred rights*'. You should read the full document to be fully empowered and enlightened.[85]

---

82   Evangelii Gaudium No 28

83   Evangelii Gaudium No 49

84   Evangelii Gaudium No 183

85   http://www.vatican.va/content/francesco/en/speeches/2014/october/documents/papa-francesco_20141028_incontro-mondiale-movimenti-popolari.html

As a means to bring the liberation and participation that he advocates, Francis endorses the role of Social Movements whom he considers as 'sowers of change, promoters of a process involving millions of actions, great and small, creatively intertwined like words in a poem'[86].

The Pope is clearly more at home hanging out with the poor and the laity than hobnobbing with the Curia whom he lambastes on a regular basis for being out of touch with reality. He also of course is not exactly popular with the hierarchy when he attacks them for their clerical culture of privilege and elitism. Francis remains an inspiration to those who seek a better world, a Church for the poor and one that is as comfortable on the streets as in the sanctuary. His every word and action are Christlike.

Orientation?

There are now 12 million Catholics in Kenya, but there has been no martyr in twenty years since John Kaiser. How could that be when we still have such inequality, impunity and endemic corruption? How long can the Church maintain cosy relationships with a system that has destroyed the morals and morale of the nation? In the event of radical change would the Church too be swept aside in a new order? These provocative questions should prompt all of us to think whether the church is really on the streets or still confined to the sanctuary.

---

86   Fratelli Tutti, No 146

Campaigns to end corruption, protect fish landing sites, affordable housing and defending the old accused of witchcraft – 2020

12

WHO OWNS THE LAND IN KENYA?

✝

The land question has dominated the Kenyan landscape for over a hundred years. The colonial government expropriated the country's most fertile land in the early 20th Century deeming it 'Crown Land' after first declaring it 'terra nullius' (land belonging to nobody). The same illegality, corruption and greed for the nation's land have continued since Kenya gained independence in 1963. The very laws, powers and opportunities that facilitated the colonial administration to acquire, distribute at will and use land as a weapon to amass wealth and maintain political control are in place today and still benefiting the current political elites, their families and their cronies.

The unaddressed and unresolved land issues continuously fester, especially around election time. Issues of historical injustice, ancestral land, inequality in settlement schemes, overcrowded informal settlements and the existence of internally displaced persons (IDPs) and squatters are found countrywide in a variety of forms. There has been a series of government commissions of inquiry established in this century to address this perennial land problem. Those commissions presented excellent reports and informed, practical recommendations but successive regimes have allowed the same reports to gather dust. There is absolutely no political will to address the issues. Land is such a hot and sensitive matter that it remains untouched - for now, that is!

The Constitution of 2010 devoted a whole chapter to land and established a National Land Commission to manage public land. But its powers have been diluted, its secretariat starved of cash and most of the first batch of its commissioners have pending criminal cases in court regarding matters of corruption and embezzlement. Somehow, the country's leadership imagine that the land issue will disappear or resolve itself and so for now the plan is to restrain protests, contain the anger and deny any injustice with the hope that in time the discontent will dissipate. That is wishful thinking as the demand and need for land remains while the huge youth population cannot all be accommodated in formal employment.

Yet, there is a much more obvious reason why the political establishment is reluctant to address the land question and that is because they themselves are the largest landowners in the country. Any proposed changes in ownership and re-distribution immediately point the finger in their direction. Sixty-seven per cent of Kenyans own less than one acre, yet the Kenyatta family alone have in their possession 500,000 acres. That acreage amounts to the size of Nyanza Region! That figure includes 15% of all beach property in the coast as well as sisal farms and ranches in Taita Taveta County and Kilifi County, not forgetting vast chunks of land in Kasarani and Thika.

But of course, they are not the only political family in possession of vast quantities of land. Former President Mwai Kibaki owns 20,000 acres in Nanyuki and another 10,000 acres in Bahati, Nakuru. His close neighbour in Bahati is the family of the late Daniel arap Moi who have another 20,000 acres as well as Kabarak Farm and a further 100,000 acres distributed between Molo and other parts of Nakuru County and Laikipia County. A trip around the best agricultural land in Kenya reveals a list of who has been who in the country's political leadership for the past half century.

The families of the country's three Presidents since independence jointly own around one million acres of the best and most valuable land in the country. But a step below them are their cronies and former Cabinet Ministers and Government officials who were granted another million acres and of course will form a vanguard in the face of any impending land redistribution demands.

While other heads of State in Africa invested in High Street properties in London and New York, or stashed their loot away in Swiss Banks or offshore accounts, that for the most part has not been the case in Kenya. The first families instead have bought for a song or allocated to themselves prime land that their citizens look upon with envy and anger every day of the week. Displaying most of your wealth before your citizens' eyes makes you quite vulnerable in times of conflict and transition. It also provides a powerful motive to retain power at all costs because a radical change of leadership would put your property and businesses in real jeopardy. That message is often not understood by the Kenyan public despite their obsession with the politics of transition.

Yet, the ongoing political dynamics in Kenya must be viewed in this context. The apparent fall out between Uhuru Kenyatta and his deputy William Ruto is not just a personality or policy clash. It is all about the issue of the Kenyatta succession in 2022. The pair were joined together in a partnership in 2013 to protect their interests and security in the International Criminal Court (ICC) cases in which both faced charges related to the electoral violence of the 2007 General Election. However, now that those charges were dropped and this arrangement gave Kenyatta a second term in State House, it is quite obvious that he and the powerful elites that support him do not trust a Ruto presidency to secure and protect their property and investments after 2022.

Raila Odinga was courted as an immediate less treacherous partner and Ruto and his allies have been side-lined ever since. In a similar vein the handshake agreement between Odinga and Kenyatta gave birth to the Building Bridges Initiative (BBI) that among other things seeks to create new executive positions through a referendum that most likely will ensure that there is some position of power for Kenyatta after he has completed his two-term presidency.

As a result, the Kenyatta and Moi families have also combined forces to protect their vested interests and most certainly not for the advancement of democracy or the implementation of the 2010 constitution. These two dynasties together with the lesser royalty of the Odinga family appear determined to retain and share power; not so much that they are natural allies but because of the uncertain consequences of not being in the top seats. The fact that the proposed Constitution of Kenya Amendment Bill of 2020 does not contain a single reference to the matter of LAND illustrates that there is absolutely no desire to address the current or historical land injustices.

They of course sooner or later must find a path to negotiate their way out of office and dispose of some of their land in a manner that will appease the Kenyan public when they no longer are in power. Kenyatta in 2016 made some gesture of generosity and placation towards squatters on his land in Njukini, Chumvini, Taita Taveta County. Initially as part of an election campaign, he promised 4,000 acres to the landless. But when the adjudication actually took place the figure was reduced to a mere 2,000 acres.

At Haki Yetu we have been documenting this case and engaging the affected community to protect their interests and rights in the whole allocation process. To the outside world it appeared like a magnanimous gesture of generosity but a closer viewing reveals a different picture altogether. Perhaps the remoteness of the land in question prevented the public from seeing the truth of what happened in the allocation process and the forceful eviction that followed.

The land in question was traditionally known as Sir Ransom Land and it was occupied by the contesting residents in 1974 after they had been evicted from nearby land known as Machungwani. They were joined by other families who returned from Tanzania and together 1,094 families occupied and farmed the land without interference for four decades. They built homes, constructed schools and churches and lived just like every other rural community in Kenya. They did not have legal title but they expected to be allocated the said land when the lease was due for renewal under the settlement schemes programme, or at least that was what their politicians and administrators had been telling them for ages.

However, much to their surprise, they were informed at a public baraza in 2015 that the Kenyatta family were the new owners of the land although the 99-year-old lease of the land had not yet expired. They were also told at a similar meeting later in the year that the Kenyattas wanted to settle the residents on a portion of the land. A nine-member committee was appointed to oversee the registration of the residents. The community was not consulted about the composition of this committee. The registration of families began and in the end 850 titles were issued although as mentioned earlier there were 1,094 families on the land, representing roughly 4,000 people. The titles were issued to the beneficiaries by Deputy President William Ruto in June 2017, just prior to the General Election.

Several of the titles had more than one family registered on them while others were allocated land that was already occupied by a completely different family. Overall, the process was unsatisfactory and a source of conflict in the community. From our records, we can prove that 221 joint titles were issued to a total of 620 families. None of these have been amended or reviewed. Those statistics reveal how chaotically the whole operation was conducted.

Our documentation shows that forty titles were not listed in the muster roll but these were allocated to staff of the Kenyatta estate that borders the disputed land as well as government officials in the area. The Ministry of Lands established a dispute tribunal mechanism but most complaints have gone unaddressed even if they were recorded. The allocation also took an ethnic dimension with local MP, Naomi Shaban ensuring that many Kamba families were denied land and replaced with those of her own Taveta community.

However, what followed the allocation exercise proved to be even more horrendous and painful to the community. In January 2018, without any prior warning or court notice, the forced eviction of the community began in the middle of the night. A contingent of police, army and vigilantes invaded and destroyed the homes that had been constructed on the land that was deemed no longer part of the settlement plan.

This callous and well-planned act demonstrated that the whole aim of the exercise was not in fact to settle and consolidate the property of the squatters but to secure the 20,000 acres that the Kenyatta family were in possession of on the adjoining land that had previously been known as Ziwani. It is currently known as Gicheha Farm and the estate includes a luxury private hotel. In fact, it is not known how the Kenyattas either acquired Gicheha Farm from former MP Basil Criticos or the Sir Ransom land either as the lease had not expired.

The eviction lasted three days and as the community were pushed backwards towards the arid, rocky parts of the settlement, the Kenyattas had another team in place that fenced off with electric wiring the property that they were not going to allow the community any access to. The perimeter fence stretches for several kilometres and the local Catholic Church now is fenced off inside the Kenyatta estate and inaccessible to the faithful. Kenyan police and Maasai herdsmen now provide security along the perimeter fence.

Then in a final stroke of destruction and contempt the first family disconnected the water to the channels and denied the farmers the opportunity to farm the land through irrigation in a manner that they had done for decades. The water comes from the River Tsavo and is a natural resource for everyone, not private property.

When the marauders departed it was discovered that several girls had been raped in the process and nine months later six unplanned infants were delivered to the community. One young man, a secondary school student, died at the hands of the police during the same operation. We also met a lady who suffered a mental breakdown as a result of the eviction and she has yet to recover, while lacking all psycho-social support.

The resulting situation is miserable and depressing. The first family dug a bore hole for the community and installed a solar immersible pump at Sir Ransom School. However much it serves the school, it is little consolation for the community who have to trek three kilometres for water that was freely available in the nearby River. Some have resorted to digging shallow wells with their bare hands.

The school itself faces many challenges. Prior to the evictions, there were 328 pupils in Sir Ransom Primary School. However, with the disruption and relocation of families that figure has now climbed to 610. There are only eight Teachers Service Commission (TSC) employees and one teacher employed by the Board of Governors for that vast number.

The case of Chumvini is a horror story. The Kenyatta family may well have genuine claims to the land – although there is no evidence available to justify that claim – but how can the president's family treat their citizens in such a brutish and callous manner? How much land does one family need? For how long can the poor tolerate violence and eviction from the hands of a government elected to serve their needs.

As I write, forty-nine families who were not allocated any land and as a result moved to the barren, rocky hills nearby have been threatened with a second round of evictions. The local administration gave them notice but after our interventions through letter writing, media highlights and lobbying the administration have begun listening to their complaints. Again, they are told that the land has "owners" but their names are not revealed. More recently we have written to Mama Ngina Kenyatta and the provincial administration to listen to the grievances of the displaced families. Besides, we have demanded that they reconnect the water from River Tsavo so that the farmers can start cultivation towards finding a way to feed their families.

This one story illustrates the gravity of the land question in Kenya. I could devote a whole book of similar injustices meted out by the powerful against the 'leftovers' all over the country. The land problem is a time bomb ready to explode anytime now. There is a limit to the patience of the poor and many are just biding their time until the opportune moment arises. Of course, it could all be avoided if there was a genuine change of heart at the top. Wishful thinking?

Victims of evictions carried out in Chumvini, Taveta, Mombasa by the First Family

13

I WRITE WHAT I LIKE AND I LIKE WHAT I WRITE

It is pretty impossible to do human rights work effectively without research, documentation and dissemination of one's findings. You may uncover massive human rights violations even investigate mega graft, but unless you are in a position to share that knowledge with the general public you cannot hope to make any impact or to be taken seriously. As the old adage goes, the pen is certainly mightier than the sword.

However, writing a press statement or publishing a report is certainly not as easy as an inexperienced hand might first imagine. We may talk at length about an issue but putting pen to paper is quite a different matter altogether. Then the subject at hand demands clarity, consistency, authenticity and bold facts to justify the claim that one may wish to make. That is not at all a simple matter and it may demand several revisits to check facts and fill in the gaps. It also requires that one writes with passion and honesty while not promoting personal grudges or agendas. Truth must be our guiding force.

Yet there are two further ingredients needed to ensure that your voice is heard. The first is access to the media and the second is locus standi or profile with the public. Neither are easily obtained and only come about through persistence, consistency and integrity. No one gains a profile overnight; it is through courageous actions, in-depth investigation, time, and independent thinking that eventually a human rights advocate is heeded.

But trying to expose injustices in faraway, remote places is particularly challenging. Thirty years ago, Turkana District had only one radio station, the national broadcaster, Kenya Broadcasting Corporation (KBC). Being the Kanu mouthpiece its primary function was to promote the ideology and popularity of President Daniel arap Moi. Every news bulletin began with the travels and activities of Moi on that particular day, whether it was going to church, opening a cattle dip, dancing with schoolgirls or sacking a cabinet minister. Mr Moi was the number one teacher, politician, farmer and pastor and the radio was there to propagate that impression.

There was no television station in Turkana either so Kenyans depended on the

BBC World Service to hear what was really going on in their own country. Listening to that news source was almost seditious so folk always looked over their shoulders as they tuned in at six in the morning and again at the same hour in the evening to listen to its Kiswahili content.

However, Turkana each day received forty copies of the Daily Nation even if it was sometimes one or two days late in arriving. The independent newspaper also had its own stringer based in Lodwar, the young and energetic Peter Kamau. Long before 'Sauti ya Jamii' and CJPC did its own publishing, Kamau was filing reports about human rights violations and abuse of office in Turkana County. His job was risky and hazardous as he was isolated and operating in an era long before the advent of email and cell phones.

We became great allies as Kamau benefited from our fax machine and we had a reliable resource through whom we could share information on the shenanigans going on in the county. Many important stories of course were never published but even the two paragraphs 'meanwhile...' news items occasionally published were enough to keep us motivated and committed to the task. Pretty soon we realised that media houses were critical partners in our work.

Upon arriving in Kitale in 1998 I soon discovered that there were half a dozen stringers based in the farming town. The relationship with them was at best ambiguous since most were not benefiting from any retainer from their media houses. They were paid according to the paragraphs submitted and published. This meant that some weeks they got very little or no income at all. However, they frequently were bribed not to submit the more revealing stories and that often proved to be more profitable. Put another way, it often benefited the journalists more in the pocket to kill a story rather than to have it published. So, they often offered our press statements to our adversaries instead of forwarding to their bureau offices in Eldoret or Nairobi.

To counteract this threat, we began to fax our stories directly to the bureaus and news desks thus bypassing the local gatekeepers. A further free and reliable source in the press was 'Letters to the Editor' which proved to be very valuable in passing on important messages and printing rejoinders on national issues without any material cost.

Packaging the messaging is of critical importance; having good media bytes and catchy headlines makes it a lot easier to garner the attention of overworked editors. All in all, it meant that we soon acquired a profile for our work in the North Rift, and media houses began to turn to us for reliable information and informed opinions. We had thus become a news source and the public wanted to read more about our work.

Arriving in Mombasa in late 2007 was like starting all over again and building fresh contacts and networks. A colleague suggested that the coast was an ecclesiastical backwater and that I would be quickly forgotten among the sandy beaches and coconut palms. However, much to my surprise, in June 2008, the Daily Nation editor, Dennis Galava, called and requested me to do a weekly column for the Saturday edition of the nation's best-selling newspaper. I thought at first it was a prank call. Eventually, realising he was genuine but feeling inadequate I hesitantly agreed to give it a go on a fortnightly basis. It was a new adventure and quite a commitment with deadlines coming every second Thursday.

Somehow, I always managed to have something of substance to say and a year later Galava called again to request if I would make it a weekly column. I agreed. This arrangement lasted for another nine years as I presented just over 400 Op-Ed columns to the Saturday Nation. During that period, I submitted from a score of countries around the globe, from coffee shops, railway stations, cyber cafes, airports and family homes. Yet, it never seemed like a chore. It was a labour of love and brought discipline and order in my work even when I was on leave.

Online abuse as well as encouragement was something that I learned to live with. No matter how caustic the comments, I made a point of acknowledging every email. Despite the obvious fact that I had a large audience to share my views with I always believed that primarily I was writing for myself. I wrestled with topics and thought long and hard before putting my views and conclusions on paper. I continuously struggled to discover my own truth and to own it before venturing to share it with others.

The first challenge, then, was to be informed and knowledgeable about the topic and this frequently involved research. Step two was to clarify my thoughts and attempt to offer sustenance and hope to the reader. To be relevant, original and authentic requires that one must also have the courage to speak truth to power. Crimes must be named and structures that are unjust or unhelpful must be called out. There was risk and anxiety associated with every article published down the years. Figures of authority in society, Church or politics may in one way or another become offended and angry with my content. That too is the price for being an honest, independent writer.

Yet at the same time humility is needed to admit that the other voice might be right, at least to some degree. One must then write with a light touch and avoid the arrogance of thinking that you have the last word. We are all pupils and disciples of Jesus or someone, so we are still learning. It is often enough to provoke debate and let the engagement continue in whatever shape it takes.

One also needs a tough skin to be a commentator or in the words of Jesus, 'to be as wise as a serpent and as gentle as a dove' (Mt 10:16). Still, honesty demands acknowledgment that Nation Media were generally very supportive and tolerant. They never interfered with the content of the commentaries, taking risks at publishing content that even they might not want to endorse. However, towards the last months of my stay at the Nation it became very evident that editorial policy, staffing and political content were changing at Nation House. Its independence was being eroded and it became much more of an instrument and mouthpiece of the governing party, Jubilee.

Dennis Galava was sacked as editor in January 2016 after writing a New Year editorial critical of President Uhuru Kenyatta.[87] Galava had been my editor for eight years. More however was to follow with the axing of renowned political economist David Ndii and the world-famous satirical cartoonist Godfrey Mwampembwa otherwise known as Gado. It became pretty obvious to me and other commentators that sooner or later we would be phased out for our independent and provocative writing. Better to jump than to be pushed we decided.

Initially, we had hand delivered a letter of concern to the Nation owner, the Aga Khan, in Geneva, Switzerland. Our correspondence was not acknowledged and it soon became clear that there was going to be no reversal of policy among the Nation Management Board.

So, in a surprise but planned move, eight commentators all resigned from Nation Media Group on a single day in March 2018. These were Maina Kiai, Rasna Warah, George Kegoro, Muthoni Wanyeki, Kwamchetsi Makokha, Gabrielle Lynch, Nic

---

87   https://www.standardmedia.co.ke/article/2000188815/nation-sacks-dennis-gala
     va-over-editorial-critical-of-president-uhuru

Cheeseman and myself.[88] My colleagues wrote not only for the Daily Nation but also for the sister publication, The East African.

The Nation group were not expecting such an embarrassing and sudden exodus as they would have preferred to weed us out one by one. They devoted a front-page editorial in their defence as well as roping in some of their few remaining columnists to launch an assault on us.[89] However, the mass resignation made news not only in Kenya but abroad[90] and despite their claims that it was business as usual, they were rattled.[91] Not only did sales plummet almost overnight but the respect with which the newspaper had been held internationally has never since been regained. It was a very damaging blow to a very wealthy and powerful media house.

However, within twenty-four hours of resigning from the Nation I received an email request from East African Standard to join Maina Kiai and George Kegoro as columnists in the Sunday Standard. Quite honestly, I would have preferred a short break from the habit of writing yet the chance to share the centre pages with my colleagues and friends was too alluring. The Standard made much of their 'new bold, fearless'[92] team as they called us and I was given more word space to share with our readers.

However, this partnership lasted just two years as I resigned from The Standard in February 2020. The last column I submitted was on February 16th and entitled, 'How can you forgive when your tormentor does not confess?'[93] Retired President Daniel arap Moi had passed away a week before and while choosing to not join the chorus of cronies and commentators who sang his praises, I wrote about the crimes from his time in power that now needed to be addressed. I deliberately toned down the message cognisant of the fact that the Moi family were the major shareholders in Standard Media.

The Standard editorial team did not publish my piece and did not contact me either.

---

88   https://citizentv.co.ke/news/nation-media-group-columnists-resign-195085/

89   https://mobile.nation.co.ke/blogs/-Columnists-RESIGNED-FROM-DAILY-NA TION/1949942-4375486-format-sitemap-14d7aek/index.html

90   https://mg.co.za/article/2018-03-27-this-suggests-state-capture-of-the-media-kenyan-columnists-speak-out/

91   https://www.theeastafrican.co.ke/news/ea/NMG-reaffirms-commitment-to-media-free dom/4552908-4360502-format-xhtml-5lf4ycz/index.html

92   https://businesstoday.co.ke/bold-standard-takes-runaway-nation-writers/

93   See Appendix

I immediately wrote to them asking for an explanation. A week passed without reply. Sunday came around again and it was not published so the following Monday morning I resigned.[94] The Managing Editor John Bowditch hurriedly replied to my correspondence requesting that I reconsider my 'resignation'. There was no suggestion that they would reconsider publishing the rejected article so I did not even bother to reply.

Thus, ended ten years of Op-Ed work. Ultimately all writers must be ready to suffer for their own beliefs and integrity. Jesus did say that the truth will set you free (John 8:32). He might have added that first it will make you miserable. But writing is a calling and a mission well worth devoting oneself to regardless of the price or consequences and I will be forever grateful to both Nation and Standard for giving me space to express my concerns for a decade. But of course, social media and in particular Twitter has opened new opportunities to continue to share concerns over important issues.

---

94 https://www.pulselive.co.ke/news/father-gabriel-dolan-resigns-from-standard-group-after-writing-about-mzee-daniel-arap/tqkmwff & https://www.kahawatungu.com/standard-columnist-gabriel-dolan-resigns/

SELECTED COLUMNS PUBLISHED IN THE *DAILY NATION* BETWEEN JULY 2008 – MARCH 2018

State must prosecute post-election violence fat cats
(October 25 2008)

In this column of September 13, I argued that the Waki commission on post-election violence had to deal decisively with impunity. Now, having waded through its 529-page report, I toast the good Mr Justice Philip Waki and declare that this is the most decisive blow struck at the culture of impunity since independence. What is remarkable about the report is that it recognises the fact that the three arms of government — the Executive, the Legislative and the Judiciary — cannot be trusted to implement the recommendations. Thus, the International Criminal Court will become the "court of last resort" should the Judiciary, Parliament and the Executive fail Kenyans as they have so frequently and contemptuously done in the past. The attorney-general's office must be an extremely disgraced government unit, as it "has promoted the sense of impunity and emboldened those who peddle the trade of violence during election periods," says the report. Not a single conviction emerged from the Akiwumi and Kiliku commissions reports. The Judiciary cannot be trusted to staff the proposed local tribunal without international support and supervision, and it is unlikely that Parliament will pass legislation establishing it to try implicated Cabinet ministers and others. Such phrases as "fragile peace", "increasing tension" and "the urgency of reconciliation" have recently been uttered to support amnesty. But then, on December 14, former UN chief Kofi Annan, who brokered the peace deal and to whom Mr Justice Waki handed the list of shame, will hand over the names of chief suspects [to] ICC prosecutor Luis Moreno-Ocampo. We can rant and rave as much as we wish about the country's sovereignty, but we must remember that Kenya is party to the ICC's Rome Statute of March 15 2005. President Kibaki freely chose to support the world court whose mandate is to intervene when the domestic judiciary does not investigate and prosecute [serious crimes] against humanity. The ICC may be poorly funded, understaffed and with a weak record on selection of cases or successful prosecutions, but it remains the greatest threat to the principal [perpetrators of violence]. The suspects should, therefore, prepare to spend some time in The Hague to await the completion of their trials. This may appear rough justice, but as Daniel Defoe once said, justice is always violent to the party offending, for every man is innocent in his own eyes. I have listened to the arguments for tempering justice with forgiveness, forgiving and forgetting and the rest. These viewpoints do not impress me for, as Annan puts it, we should not protect perpetrators for the sake of peace. Sure, we all want peace, but the peace we have been enjoying is only a brief interlude between general elections. Peace must be accompanied by justice to ensure that the 2012 elections are the first peaceful ones in more than two decades. Too often we have been contrasting peace and justice as incompatible goals. However, they are two sides of the same coin. We cannot have peace without justice, nor justice without peace. Retributive justice is often presented as the direct opposite of forgiveness. But retributive justice is often a stage on the road to forgiveness. Let me explain this by way of an example. On May 13, 1981, Pope John Paul II was shot and critically wounded by a deranged assassin, Mehmet Ali Agca. The attacker was immediately arrested and sentenced to life imprisonment. Two days after Christmas of 1983, the Pope visited Agca in his prison cell and "spoke to him as a brother whom I have pardoned". Although the sentence continued, the victim had reconciled with the assailant. What are the key elements in this story? The State has a duty to prose-cute and sentence when serious crimes have taken place, and forgiveness is the choice, duty and frequently the victim's burden. Put another way, it is not the duty of the State to grant forgiveness or amnesty, nor is it the victim's right to revenge. These are the basic tenets of law, but they appear not to be understood by Kenyan MPs. For the record, Agca spent 19 years in an Italian jail and was then transferred to Turkey for sentencing on another charge, but granted parole in 2006. Duty to victims: The State has a duty to the victims of the post-election violence. It must uncover the truth of what happened and seek justice for the victims by prosecuting and sentencing the perpetrators. Later, reparations need to be made to the victims. The State must permanently remove from office all the people named by the Waki commission. Legislators are paid to uphold the principles of the rule of law, and they have no business talking of forgiveness or amnesty. Nobody but the victim can grant forgiveness, and no one has the right to forgive on behalf of another. Why is it so difficult to face these truths in Kenya? Why do we find it so unaccept-able or unimaginable that prominent Kenyans should spend time behind bars for orchestrating and funding the commission of crimes? Are we afraid that they might unleash further violence on us should we question their culpability? Or are the handful of suspects holding the country to ransom? We must be honest and admit that, for decades, we have been sweeping so much dirt under the carpet. And now the carpet has almost reached the roof and soon it may blow the roof off our home. It is neither an embarrassment nor a shame to admit that we need outside help to clean up the house. The Waki commission has set the standard and shown us the way. If it bites the bullet and implements the report, Kenya will be a more peaceful, just and progressive country. And, in a few short years, we will be asking ourselves why it took us so long to face the demon of impunity.

The reality of living in a gatekeeper country
(January 31 2009)

Civil servants are expected to rest during weekends. So, you can imagine how surprised I was to be invited by the District Commissioner for a leaders' meeting on a Sunday afternoon. And there was only one item [on the] agenda — the food crisis in the area — and the matter was urgent. The hall was thronged when the meeting was called to order. Strategic positions were taken up, where one could gain sight of the chair's eye and access to the passing microphone. I learned the ground rules for survival and participation at such meetings many years ago. Amazingly, things have not changed much since. When it comes to food distribution, and most development issues for that matter, the village elders and politicians still dominate and retain their posts as community "gatekeepers". Controlled entry: Historically, they may have played a protective — even consultative — role. However, with the arrival of the colonial settlers, wazee wa mtaa were appointed gate-keepers of a gatekeeper administration. Since then, they have controlled entry into the community, its information and resources. If you want access to the people, you must pass through them, and they have the powers to either lock you out or grant you admission. At public forums you may also be treated to the sight of women and youth leaders, but don't be fooled; these are usually the elders' second wives and offspring. These figures are entrenched in their positions and the provincial administrators are happy to permit their excesses because they will always remain loyal to the state. Village elders are the loyalists of today. That Sunday afternoon I was reminded of how undemocratic and unrepresentative our decision-making organisations are. Not only do they determine who gets relief and who goes hungry, but another cadre of them controls development funds. I ponder our list of Constituency Development Fund (CDF) committee members. They are not just hand-picked, they are also damned incestuous and, I fear, fairly typical of what you will find elsewhere. With such control of the nation's resources is it any wonder that 10 million of Kenya's population need food relief? If the coalition government has left 25 per cent of the nation hungry in its first year, are we not likely to have 99 per cent in poverty by 2012? Let us not blame God or the weather, global recession or anything else. What I am suggesting simply and plainly is that bad governance, corruption and lack of accountable institutions produce famine, and ours is made by this government. This is not a new or radical idea. Ten years ago, Indian economist Amartya Sen won the Nobel Prize for economics. His principal thesis was that large-scale famines have never happened in functioning democracies. The key word here is "functioning" because what we have here in Kenya is a purely administrative democracy. An effective democracy is concerned with transparency, opportunities, information, accountability and the rule of law - [attributes our leaders do not have]. Sen showed how thousands can starve even when a country's food production has not diminished. Last week, Catholic bishops posed the question why [are we] are importing large quantities of maize when farmers in the North Rift are keeping large quantities which they cannot sell because of the miserable prices offered by the National Cereals and Produce Board? Agriculture Minister William Ruto tried to convince us that imported food costs less, but transport and handling charges push up the price. We all know that, so why not give our own farmers decent prices instead of funding multi-national oil and transport companies and a politically correct grain handling company in Mombasa? We cannot eat democracy, for sure, but autocracy makes us starve, and death by hunger is just another form of state genocide. Which brings me back to the gatekeepers. What I witnessed at the district level is for the most part replicated all the way to the top. This government is a coalition of gatekeepers and we live in a gatekeeper state. People at the helm control entry and access to the nation's wealth and resources, while managing the information around their misdeeds. They dismiss, forgive, rehabilitate and remain as before. Like the village elders, most of them are old and male. So, expect limited reforms as their major concern is regime survival. A friend of mine suggests that the top gatekeepers are like game hunters who loot and plunder as a sport and boast aloud of their achievements at Parliament bars. They have become illegitimate game-keepers as their positions are based on greed. So, what can we do? We have three choices. The first is to give up hope and confine our concerns to our families, professions and businesses. Regretfully and shamefully, the middle class has mostly taken this option, which is no choice at all. The second is that we can plan to participate in, penetrate, subvert and transform the structures that have become corrupt. I once witnessed the impact of such a strategy in Turkana district when the "Kanu zone" philosophy was confronted and dismantled by groups of young activists in the mid-1990s. The final choice then comes with the realisation that the gatekeeper coalition cannot save this country, so we urgently need a new movement and a new beginning. That is where you come in.

Grand corruption is [a] crime against humanity
(March 3 2009)

Last month, the United Kingdom Serious Fraud Office announced that it had stopped investigating the $750 million (about Sh60 billion) Anglo Leasing scandal. It cited reasons for its withdrawal as Attorney-General Amos Wako's failure to cooperate with its inquiries and his reluctance to give evidence. One sympathises with the office over its frustration. But this is until we recall that Prime Minister Tony Blair also halted investigations in 2006 into the corruption scandal involving Prince Bandar of Saudi Arabia and British arms giant British Aerospace (BAE). Millions of dollars were paid by the Department of Defence as backhanders to the Saudi prince as part of a $70 billion arms deal. Mr Blair announced in parliament that the investigations would have harmed the national interest. There is a familiar ring about that pronouncement. Corruption is found everywhere and this continent certainly does not have the monopoly. But what is particular about Kenyan corruption is that there is a link between the vice and endemic poverty, hardships and suffering. Kenya is not a poor country, but one that has been impoverished by organised political theft. There is [a] close relationship between the plunder of the nation and the people's pain. When families spend their lives in tiny rooms and take three weeks to raise funds to bury their loved ones; when your neighbours are deprived of anti-retrovirals because billions from the Global Fund for Aids is unaccounted for; when casual workers earn Sh300 for [a] 14-hour day's work and spend Sh2 to watch the evening news bulletin and how the grand coalition has robbed them; then you know that grand corruption is a crime against humanity. When hundreds of thousands cannot access secondary [school] education then you know that the heavens cry out for justice. Believe it or not, Mr Kiraitu Murungi was the first person to declare that grand corruption was a crime against humanity. The venue was Seoul, South Korea, and the year 2003. It was just one year before the exposure of the Anglo Leasing scandal, three years before the John Githongo tapes were released and long before the Sh7.6 billion Triton scandal. Shamefully, the Rome statute does not define grand corruption as a crime against humanity. Transitional justice therefore gives attention to traditional human rights abuses and leaves social injustice to the post-transitional reform era. This is shown by the fact that of 34 truth commissions held around the world be- tween 1974 and 2005, only three recognised the intrinsic link between human rights violations and economic crimes. Yet corruption feeds and funds impunity. This fact was acknowledged by the East Timor truth commission that calculated that 84,200 of the 102,800 victims had died of hunger and illness rather than being killed outright, or forcibly disappeared during the Indonesian occupation. Should our own truth commission not do a similar audit and find out the number of people who have died of hunger, poverty and neglect caused by the looting of the nation's wealth? This requires that the commission provides an accurate and complete list of plunderers, data on the wealth amassed and make recommendations for recovery. In the process the commission must ensure that recovered wealth is used for reparations and rebuilding the nation. Article 79 of the Rome statute states that victims may obtain reparations from the trust fund for victims and does allow for forfeiture of proceeds, property and assets derived directly from crimes. The truth commission could start by revisiting the Kroll report that gives accurate information on how Sh130 billion was looted and invested in banks and property in 28 countries. The Ndung'u report is another reliable source. Kenya Land Alliance has shown how 1,189 acres of the Karura forest cost the Treasury Sh8 billion, while it would cost a mere Sh7.5 billion to employ the required 33,000 primary school teachers. Last week, President Kibaki told of plans to build 560 secondary schools before 2012. All of them could be completed with the Sh7.6 billion looted in the oil scandal. This money must be recovered, or will investigations be dropped and amnesty granted after another Damascus-like conversion by Brother "Paul" Devani? The first revision of the International Criminal Court statute takes place this year. Would it not be appropriate for the Kenya National Commission on Human Rights to launch a campaign to have Article 7 amended to include grand corruption as a crime against humanity? The Waki envelope contains a list of perpetrators of crimes against humanity. If the ICC statute is amended to include corruption as a crime against humanity, we could soon be sending another list of names to ICC prosecutor Luis Moreno Ocampo. Do not be surprised, then, to discover that several names will appear on both lists.

No more imposed heroes for the country
(October 23 2010)

No more Moi Day, and I didn't hear a single complaint about its removal. I decided to mark the day anyhow with a visit to Ken Matiba's hotels on Diani beach. Just one of the group's three hotels remains open, and that is thanks to the initiative and endeavour of a few loyal staff. It is hard to pardon the Nyayo regime for destroying a man's health and business. Yet Kenneth Matiba remains a hero for many. His resignation as a Cabinet minister in December 1988 in protest over the rigged elections of the same year was an act of defiance. His principled resistance was the first nail in the coffin of the one-party state. Saba Saba will always remain a revered day for Kenyans, even as kumi kumi is discarded to the dustbin of history like the equally dangerous brew that shares the name. Kenyatta Day is no more either. Instead, we have one National Mashujaa Day. As the nation searches for meaningful celebrations for national figures, Kenyans must ensure that the state systems no longer impose national heroes on the public. Kenyans everywhere must be allowed to identify and nominate those they themselves wish to [feast] and remember. For decades, national awards on public holidays have been dished out to loyalists, [cronies, businesspeople] and politicians of ill repute. If a decent and deserving person was honoured, it meant little due to the strange sounding title and infamous company that went with the award. Rather than bringing honour, most such awards were associated with shame and sycophancy. Yes, we all need heroes in our lives, yet, as Ernest Hemingway once said, it is harder to have heroes as you get older but it is sort of necessary. Heroes and heroines remind us of the divine call within us all to serve and do what is right regardless of the cost. I guess that is why we have more dead martyrs than living heroes. The new Constitution has given us the new holiday but it also gave us Chapter 6 on Leadership and Integrity. If any person does not meet the standards set by that chapter, they deserve neither recognition nor honour. Indeed, if awards have been awarded to individuals who can no longer pass the integrity test, then they should be stripped of that accolade forthwith. Kenya is not short of heroes. We will not find many of them in the ruling class but we will find them in all walks of life and in every county. In some cases, they may not even be known outside their own village. Yet they inspire us by their courage, integrity, honesty and service. They all remind us what dignity and beauty are even in the face of cynicism, greed and corruption. But even heroes need encouragement. Let the weekend not pass without acknowledging the heroes in our lives. We can do so by a simple prayer, visit or word of gratitude. At the same time, you will be acknowledging that you too are called to greatness.

Did Pope let the genie out of the bottle?
(December 4 2010)

I meet HIV positive people every day as they collect ARVs or attend their support group meetings. The poor cannot afford time for shame, stigma or despair. They may have their low moments but the demands of a hard life compel them to pick themselves up quickly and attend to their families' needs. I am pleased that our church contributes up to 35 per cent of all HIV treatment and care in Kenya. The compassionate and merciful mission of the Gospel message is found in quality health service in the most remote and poorest of places. Many church personnel have also taken a pragmatic pastoral approach to health care, making condoms available to couples at high risk of infecting each other. Yet, frequently there is inconsistency in both approach and accessibility to condoms. Giving them selectively or under the table - lest the hierarchy disapprove - makes protection against infection a privilege rather than a right or moral responsibility. Such cautious practices also suggest that using condoms may be illicit and immoral, further adding to the stigma. At the same time some health units have a complete 'condom ban'. What has been absent is a consistent, open policy and that is primarily due to unclear guidelines coming from the Vatican. Over forty years ago, Pope Paul VI taught that condoms as a contraceptive devise were immoral as they denied the possibility of creating new life. That was before the Aids pandemic. Now what if condoms could be used to prevent the transmission of an early death through infection with Aids? Could condoms not be a pro-life tool or a prophylactic to prevent transmission among high-risk groups? For two decades the Vatican has been silent on whether condoms could ever be an acceptable means of reducing transmission. Now Pope Benedict has made a small concession by admitting that condom use is acceptable in exceptional cases to prevent the spread of Aids. It may be a small step but the Pope is clearly stating that compassion, prudence and mercy should be the guiding principles in our approach to Aids. He teaches moral responsibility for our actions and continues that 'fixation on the condom implies the banalisation of sexuality'. How true. He is not suggesting that condoms can solve the problem of Aids; nor is he advocating the right to casual or recreational sex. However, the church too could be accused of being obsessed with the issue of condoms. Perhaps it needs to recover the beauty of teaching on sexuality, love and responsible behaviour. Condoms alone will certainly not solve the problem of Aids. Abstinence and fidelity must continue to be promoted as virtues that are desirable and attainable. However, responsible behaviour also includes the moral duty to plan our families and placing a blanket 'condom ban' on couples is a burden that has alienated many Christians. The Pope's concession may have, inadvertently or intentionally, let the genie out of the bottle and reopened the whole debate on condoms. But in the meantime, church health workers should at last be open and free to make condoms available as part of its comprehensive treatment for people with Aids.

Did you offer prayers for the Ocampo Six?
(April 9 2011)

Did you lead your congregation in prayers for the Ocampo Six, a friend asked me the other day? Another colleague claims he prayed that they would never return so that the media circus would end and we could resume building the nation. We are an extremely religious nation, and prayers and crusades are available on every street corner for every occasion. Priests and pastors, through their anointing and laying on of hands, have played a key colluding role in converting The Hague Six from suspects into victims and martyrs. We have seen evangelists, moderators and preachers of all descriptions, age and gender lining up in stadiums all over the country with outstretched arms and raised voices like a bunch of religious cheer-leaders. I was hardly surprised for most Christian churches have long since been compromised and co-opted as religious actors in our dysfunctional society. The entire political elite in Kenya benefits from a Christianity-induced impunity. Churches also benefit from the culture of patronage through harambees and appointments to just about every commission of inquiry. In the process, churches have abandoned their calling and lost their independence. We now have lots of pastors and priests, but almost no prophets to warn us of the threats to our fragile peace. Who then can read the signs of the times and offer challenges and hope to the multitudes? The warning signals are there for what have been billed as prayer meetings [but] are mere camouflage for spreading ethnic hatred. The Vice-President told the nation in Nakuru that detaining the Ocampo Six would lead to an outbreak of violence. That sounds like a threat and a promise. The Prime Minister's personal attacks on some of the accused are equally dangerous and irresponsible. Our politicians are playing with fire and no one is crying halt, least of all religious leaders. Are they going to remain silent and indifferent until 2013 and then deliver another round of apologies for failing to show visionary leadership as the politicians again prepared for war? Yes, everyone needs prayers for God does not have favourites, but do remember to "set your mind on God's kingdom and his justice first, and the rest will come to you as well" (Mt 6:33). True religion is caring for the widow and orphans and the IDPs for "to know God is to do justice for the oppressed" (Jeremiah 22:15). The God I believe in cannot be manipulated, bribed, threatened, evicted or deceived and that God isn't short of cash either. Preachers promising miracles to politicians are mere charlatans for hire. Yet there are enough decent religious leaders to prevent bloodshed and curb politicians if only they would rise to the challenge. The Franciscan Family following the great peace and ecumenical model, Francis of Assisi, will spend a week fasting and praying for justice for the victims at Freedom Corner beginning tomorrow afternoon. Civil Society have organised their own event for today and tomorrow at Uhuru Park. Maybe you could join them for an hour or a day, and show the political elite what true religion is all about.

Why principals skipped the May Day fete
(May 7 2011)

I wonder why the two Principals once again skipped this year's Labour Day Celebrations. Did they fear mud balls — or worse — being hurled in their direction? Is it shame at the appalling failure to implement the labour laws and improve the lot of the working poor; or is it just reluctance to admit that our limited economic growth primarily results from the exploitation of our labour force? Whatever the case, Labour Minister John Munyes cut a lonely figure as the nation's workers boycotted or walked out of the global holiday that should honour the service and ingenuity of our workers. It is hardly a surprise that workers reacted angrily to the 12.5 per cent increase in the minimum salary when basic foodstuffs have increased by 25 percent since January. Fifty MPs trooped off to The Hague to support their colleagues while there were less than 10 in Parliament on Wednesday to discuss the soaring cost of living! We face not only dehumanising and endemic poverty, but a poverty of respect and belief in the working Kenyan. Worse still, the working poor are blamed for most of our ills: overcrowded slums, urban crime and out of control population growth. Labourers are considered beasts of burden that move the nation's goods in mkokoteni (hand carts) rather than assets who deserve respect and reward for their hard work. Poverty then is like punishment for a crime you didn't commit. Both the private sector and the associations of manufacturers and employers warned the government that increasing the minimum wage would cause further inflation, discourage investors and add to the unemployment figures. Such scare tactics are mere camouflage for their own greed. The truth is that failure to listen to the grievances of workers will surely lead to social unrest. Besides, giving a decent living wage to all workers will increase their spending power and boost the economy as they invest in better housing, facilities and health care for their families. Put another way, we all benefit from a workforce that is treated well. Yet in Kenya, we imagine that we can only prosper through corruption, crime or exploitation as there is not enough wealth to satisfy 40 million. So, our society has become a greedy, cruel and harsh one, very much like the story of the rich man and Lazarus in Luke 16. In the parable the poor man survives from the crumbs and leftovers that fall from the rich man's table. Yet the horrifying lesson is that even if someone should rise from the dead, the excessively rich will not change their attitudes and contempt for the Lazaruses of this world. People rarely change voluntarily and that is why we have governments and parliaments whose role is to distribute justly the nation's wealth while focusing on the common good. If the misery, the deprivation, of the working poor is caused not by the forces of nature but by our institutions, attitudes and legislation, then we in turn have the capacity to correct, reform and transform our society by institutions, policies and laws that recognise, as Plato did, that the poor peasant and the mighty prince are equally dear to God.

Truth team must summon Moi to testify
(June 4 2011)

The Truth, Justice and Reconciliation Commission (TJRC) appears to be directing most of its energy towards uncovering the truth about the Wagalla Massacre of 1984. The moving testimony of victims and survivors of that brutal event was recently complemented by the evidence of Northern Kenya Development Minister Mohamed Elmi, who tearfully recalled how as a young nurse he tried to rescue and treat hundreds of victims. He combed bushes and manyattas looking for the injured together with one Anna Lena Tonelli, a Catholic volunteer from Italy. Ms Tonelli was a lawyer by profession but spent 35 years working with the Somali community as a medic. An extraordinary Christian who dressed and lived like local Somali women, she had a particular devotion to treatment of TB patients. She was the first to document evidence of the atrocity and claimed there was a government plot "to commit genocide against the Degodia community". Her writings tell how Degodia men were rounded up, stripped naked, shot dead and chemicals poured on their corpses. Ms Tonelli estimated that over 1,000 people were eliminated in the Wagalla atrocity. For her efforts to assist the injured and to expose the genocide, she was deported a year later by the Moi Government. No human rights group, however, investigated the atrocity. Anna Lena relocated to Borama in Somalia in late 1985 where she established a TB Hospital. But she predicted that "no evil ever remains hidden, and no truths remain unrevealed ... one day goodness will shine forth". If there is a season for everything, then this must be the right time to address the slaughter. The TJRC has listed a number of senior government people summoned to testify. Most opted not to appear in Wajir, but are expected to testify in Nairobi this week. Chief among them is Bethuel Kiplagat, whose only role in the TJRC henceforth will be as a witness and not as its chairperson. He has been negatively mentioned by former Australian ambassador Zakayo Kamenchu, who claimed that Mr Kiplagat attended a security meeting in Wajir prior to the massacre and later briefed diplomatic staff on damage control after revelations of the slaughter became known. The TJRC will almost certainly be calling more witnesses to shed light on this dark incident. The TJRC Act of 2008 Article 6(e) states that their mandate includes "to investigate and determine whether the violations and abuses were deliberately planned and executed by the state". Sooner or later, then, the commission will have to consider summoning Mr Moi to give his version of events. Article 7 of the Act states that anyone can be summoned and even compelled to attend a session. However, if Mr Moi were to voluntarily come forward and tell us the truth, that magnanimous gesture would go a long way towards acknowledgment, closure and reconciliation with the Somali community. Anna Lena Tonelli cannot appear as she was brutally assassinated at her hospital in Borama on October 5, 2003 but she would rejoice in heaven to see justice for her beloved people.

Would infant Jesus find a home in Kenya? (December 24 2011)

The past year could be considered the Year of Protest. Starting with the April Spring in Egypt, Libya and Tunisia, we have witnessed regime change take place at an alarming rate in societies totally unaccustomed to popular uprisings. The global recession has also given rise to a spate of occupation protests in 900 cities worldwide. While the former protests have focused on basic democratic rights, the latter have demanded more direct democracy in societies where citizens experience the frustration of being dominated by bankers never voted into office. The London protest has gained particular notoriety as the protest camp is located at the doorsteps of the famous St Paul's Cathedral. Initially the protest led to the closure of the cathedral and the subsequent resignation of Canon Giles Fraser, who felt that the church should not only accommodate the protesters but facilitate debate on issues of justice, poverty and corporate greed. The tension that followed in the Church of England is really about two models of church; the church as an institution with buildings decorated to adorn and honour the sacred and the notion of church as a movement of people inspired by a gospel message of justice and change. The Cathedral houses sacred art and architecture while the protesters lived nearby in tents. Then again St Paul was a tentmaker and one image of the Christmas event is that of the Son of God pitching his tent amid humanity. Which of course beggars the question as to where would Jesus more likely be found — among the sacred arches of the cathedral or among the crowded, chaotic tent site of the protesters?

Bring the metaphor a little nearer home and we might wonder where Jesus would choose to be born tonight in Kenya: among the IDPs who have been in tents for four years; among the demolished homes and informal settlements of forgotten Kenyans or among our troubled and unemployed youth? Would our churches recognise him or would they be looking for him only in their houses of worship? Would his birth be first made known by angels to Samburu pastoralists displaced from their ancestral land by foreigners and a retired politician all in the name of conservation? We can only guess but never grasp the mind of God. Yet God Almighty chose to be born in a smelly cowshed in a land under occupation. God abandoned pristine holiness and immersed himself in the dirt and pain of the human condition. He opened hearts and homes and excluded no-one. Churches are getting bigger and louder each day in Kenya. Many anointed leaders have retreated to their sanctuaries secure in their robes and rites, with doors and minds closed to debate on hard questions that trouble our nation about ethnicity, the Ocampo Six, endemic poverty, alarming inequality, a foolish war and a disturbing ballot. Many churches are more concerned about private schools than public engagement, thus becoming more exclusive and ghettoish by the day. The man who came to comfort the afflicted also afflicted the comfortable. Our churches are comfy in their organisation, secure in their traditions but frequently irrelevant to the millions for whom life is short, painful and brutish. Peace to God's people on earth!

Time to resist politicians' bullying tactics ((February 25 2012)

Last week, a woman told me she prays for Uhuru Kenyatta and William Ruto every day. She has even graced some of their "prayer rallies". It later emerged that my friend, Lillian, is far more pragmatic than devout. She and her family were burnt out of their farmstead in 1992, 1997 and again in 2007 and she cannot bear the thought of another eviction in 2012. Her rather simple analysis is that a G2 – in her words – combination for the presidency is the best guarantee that she will not be a victim of ethnic-political violence this time around. The ethnic balance is just right, she believes. If such views are representative, and such conclusions consistent, then democracy has taken on a whole new worrying shape in Kenya. Your personal safety has become far more important than your personal choice and fear, rather than conviction, may now determine where you mark the ballot paper. In many cases, you may not even vote at all. Many women tell me that they will relocate upcountry with their children for two months around election time and leave their men-folk to protect the family businesses. They claim no matter how they vote; they always end up with rogues and gangsters anyhow; so, no big deal if they fail to cast their ballot. It reminded me of another acquaintance, Joey from Liberia, whom I met 15 years ago and who taught me the intrigues of election campaigning in his home country. Charles Taylor campaigned in 1997 on the chilling slogan, 'he killed my Ma, he killed my Pa, I will vote for him,' and in the process terrorised 75 per cent of the population into voting for him. In plain language, Taylor was telling Liberians he would resume the war if they did not vote for him. Ellen Johnson Sirleaf was the runner-up with a mere 10 per cent of the "popular" vote. We have not yet reached that level of intimidation and insecurity in Kenya but we must exercise extreme caution to avoid chaos. I have no strong opinions as to whether the G2 should stand together, separately or not at all in the 2012 elections. But their weekly rallies do appear designed to force the hands of Kenyans into allowing the two ICC accused to appear on the ballot sheet. That is disturbing. If the ICC accused bully their way on to the ballot paper, then they can in turn intimidate Kenyans into voting for them. Should that scenario develop, then it must be resisted. Both Mr Kenyatta and Mr Ruto have said they will ensure the violence and destruction of 2007 will not be repeated this year. That sounds comforting but that guarantee must be unconditional. In other words, whether they are candidates or holed up in Holland, they must be seen to uphold the rule of law and respect free choice. To date we have not heard of that type of commitment. Besides, Kenyans are well aware of the hate speech propagated by their juniors at some rallies. They would well be advised to remember that Charles Taylor is currently keeping his peace in The Hague while Ellen Johnson and Joey live comfortably in Monrovia. What can Lillian hope for?

We are the ones we have been waiting for
(March 3 2012)

I usually advise foreign visitors to watch the evening news so that they get an interesting perspective on the concerns and hopes of the nation. However, I always add a word of caution that the bad news comes in the first half of the bulletin while the second part generally contains the more hopeful tidings. Put another way, the first segment is mostly about political intrigues and malicious power games just like a continuation of the Mexican soap operas that precede the news bulletins. The second part is about the real Kenya: full of human-interest stories, and some remarkable achievements in the worlds of business, development and sports. Unfortunately, political elites not only dominate the media space, but also steal from the coffers, impoverish the nation, and determine when we will live in peace and go to war. They have the means and resources to turn the nation into a battle field every five years, so that elections are times of dread. In one corner, we have two schoolyard bullies, hell bent on bringing the nation to its knees and pretending that that is a prayerful position. They crisscross the nation warning voters should they dare vote against them, then Kenyans will live — or perhaps die — to regret it. Intimidation characterises their version of democracy. In the other corner, we have a party where acclamation, anointing by tribal chieftains and a general culture of 'toshacracy' are presented as their unique form of democracy. The two opponents have already started slugging it out and before the year is finished, they may have punched each other drunk. The culture then that drives our politics is little different from that of the Mafia of Sicily or Chicago, with the same requirements of family and blood binding such groups together. Political parties are not designed to represent public interests but are clandestine racketeering enterprises protecting their loot and sharing out the dirty deals. This analysis could be quite depressing and fatalistic were you to just view the first sordid segment and forget the good news that is frequently ignored. Kenya has huge potential for alternative leadership from among the business and private sectors as well as the arts, academia, banking and ICT domains. There are many Kenyans of integrity and ability who are globally recognised but almost unknown at home. Yet, rather than summoning them to leadership, we all await a Messiah of Mandela proportions. That will certainly not happen. Instead, we must realise that we are the ones we are waiting for. As Gandhi stated, you must become the change that you want. You must step forward and realise that Kenyans deserve better leadership and that the potential for generational and transformative change is right before your eyes. For half a century we have been addicted to bad leadership. We must end that dependency and spend the holy period of Lent reflecting on what each can do to kickstart the change that most want so badly

The poor live in constant fear of eviction
(April 21 2012)

We wasted our time voting for a new Constitution; it was just another political trick to confuse us so that they could demolish our homes in the middle of the night. That was the desperate lament of 75-year-old Mama Lucia, one of the 203 family heads whose homes were destroyed last Saturday morning in Kibarani informal settlement in Mombasa. Demolitions are always grotesque. When they are illegal and affect people whom you know and love, they are all the more painful, depressing and enraging. How can common people resist two giant bulldozers, 200 riot police and a similar number of militias? There was no court order, no notice, no court bailiff and, above all, no mercy. The sight of the militia leaving the scene of destruction on police vehicles from Makupa and Changamwe police stations would be almost incredible if I did not have the evidence. The Ocampo Four are facing charges in The Hague of hiring militia to evict and displace Kenyans in 2007. Five years later, Mombasa police parade and ferry their own militia with impunity and leave behind another 1,000 IDPs in their wake. What is the difference? No wonder the police are resisting reform. All the more painful for the victims is the fact that the private developer who claims ownership of the land is an English businessman. Saturday's evictions were like a repetition of a scene from the 1950s with white settlers deploying hired militia and home guards to evict local landless people. As we celebrate 50 years of independence it is only right and urgent to ask what has really changed. How can the rights of one foreigner to purchase property surpass those of 1,000 poor Kenyans who have lived there for over 20 years? This is not the first illegal eviction to take place recently in Mombasa. In December last year, 100 families were evicted from Dunga Nusu and another 150 from Mishomoroni. Over 150,000 people live in informal settlements in Mombasa. Their situation is precarious and they live in daily dread of evictions. They have no faith in this coalition government's willingness to protect and settle them. We talk of Vision 2030, a new port and improved railways, but for the poor the legacy of this coalition is surely that of evictions. The coalition came to birth after 650,000 Kenyans had been displaced and the trend has continued ever since. More illegal and unmerciful evictions have taken place under this administration than any other since independence. What this leadership fails to understand is that you cannot bulldoze the poor into oblivion. They are not obstacles to development but a greater untapped and more powerful resource than the oil discovered in Turkana. As long as land grabbers have godfathers, we will witness a similar degree of illegal acquisitions and evictions in 2012 as in the final year of Mr Moi's regime in 2002. But be warned that the poor will fight back as they did on Monday in Kibarani, when they evicted the police and the bulldozer.

Church stand on family planning outdated
(July 21 2012)

Wednesday is vaccination day at our clinic. Last week, I met five young mothers rushing to have their bundles of joy face the needle. There is great pleasure in providing such a needy and important service. But that satisfaction dissipated when I discovered that all five women were under 20 years of age, and none of them had a husband. They may still become terrific parents, but given a choice would most of them have delayed parenthood until such time as they were ready and able to give their children a good start in life? Besides, should the Church not offer services on family planning, as well [as] pre-and post-natal care, if genuinely committed to advancing the health of mothers and children? We are now seven billion on planet earth, and we seem to have fulfilled the Creator's command to fill the earth a long time ago. The earth can sustain such numbers if we all learned to share its great resources but the issue is just not about statistics and wealth distribution but about the health and welfare of mothers and their offspring. Kenya had a population of 8.6 million at independence but by 1979 that figure had risen to 15.3 million and is now at 41 million and increasing by a million each year. At this rate there will be 64 million Kenyans to celebrate Vision 2030. Is that sustainable? Most women it would appear just want a little space and time between one child and another. That is the view of billionaire philanthropist Melinda Gates, wife of Bill and mother of three children aged 10, 13 and 16. She is a practicing Catholic but when it comes to Church teaching on family planning, she claims that bishops say one thing but ordinary Catholics do another. In USA, 82 percent of Catholics say contraception is morally acceptable. Ms Gates' concern is not letting women and babies die and that she believes is more important than arguing about what type of contraceptive is right. As a result, the Gates Foundation will invest $560 million in the next eight years on research to develop safer contraceptives with fewer side effects. She says that it takes a woman to speak out on these issues, and she does have a point. Many church facilities already provide condoms to couples to prevent the spread of HIV. But that is often done secretly and quietly, that is not preaching what they practice. As a result, beneficiaries are often made to feel deviant or guilty for apparently opposing church teaching. Yet here contraceptives are intended to prevent HIV transmission and protect life, so could that be deemed "sinful"? Should family planning services, too, not be provided as standard practice in church health facilities so that women are given the right information to make the best choices on planning their families in a responsible and loving manner? Women are not mere baby making machines. God made them in His/Her likeness and gave them wisdom, compassion and discernment to be responsible parents. Is it not time that men started listening to them and that the church revisited its own ideas on family planning?

Court ruling on hijab a blow to diversity (September 29 2012)

Last week, Lady Justice Cecilia Githua ruled that 48 Muslim girls in Kenya High School did not have the right to wear the hijab (religious headscarf) as part of their school uniform. In giving the ruling on Judicial Review 318 of 2010, the judge declared that a circular of July 2009 by then Education permanent secretary Karega Mutahi permitting the hijab was illegal as only a minister has the power to make such a directive in interpreting the Education Act. The judge went on to argue that there was no discrimination in the national school as Muslims are free and facilitated to practise their religion and they also are granted the opportunity to study Islamic Religious Education (IRE) as an examinable subject. Moreover, the Education Act Cap 211 allowed school boards to select a suitable uniform for all pupils with the specific aim of bringing harmony, equality and cohesion among the student population. Now allowing 48 girls to dress and look differently would be considered preferential treatment by the other pupils and they in turn might make their own demands. The judge said that "nothing represents equality more than school uniforms". The judge's argument is consistent and clear but hardly convincing. Muslim students may have freedom of worship but when they are not allowed to don the hijab — the normal religious and cultural attire for Islamic girls — then they may well feel that their religious rights are ignored or denied. A hijab could hardly cause offence to non-Muslims and might well enhance the appearance of the school uniform. However, the real argument of the judge is that one is free to practise religious beliefs but not to express them through attire. If you apply that principle on a general basis then students should not be allowed to wear crosses, rosaries or other religious items while in the school compound. Moreover, if that ruling is applied to all public institutions, we might well go down the road the French chose in 2004 when they banned the hijab, Jewish skullcaps and Christian crosses not only from schools but from all public institutions. Their argument was that

France is a secular society with no preference given to any religion. However, the reality is that secularists have made the right to freedom of religion to become a freedom from religion, where rights to publicly express faith are denied and religion can only comfortably express itself in private. Currently, a British Airways check-in worker is fighting her case in the European Court for unfair dismissal for refusing to remove her cross at work. Kenya is a very diverse, pluralist society confirmed in the preamble of the Constitution which states: "Proud of our ethnic, cultural and religious diversity, and determined to live in peace and unity as one indivisible sovereign nation." The decision of Judge Githua was a blow to pluralism, tolerance, diversity and cohesiveness in the country. It will surely be challenged in the Court of Appeal. The French nation was founded on the three principles of Liberty, Equality and Fraternity. The latter has been replaced with conformity. Kenya must celebrate its diversity and honour its differences as its way to nation building.

It's back to basics for Catholic Church
(March 30 2013)

Pope Francis pays his bills, rides in a saloon car and told his kith and kin not to bother travelling from Argentina for his installation. He advised them to give the money to the poor. Jorge Mario Bergoglio was accustomed to riding in Buenos Aires buses and is reported to have purchased tickets to travel on Rome matatus. A further nightmare for his handlers is that he has avoided the Papal Palace. Yet, it appears security services will have to quickly adapt to their new boss rather than the other way round. A leader who is a beacon of simplicity and poverty is now dismantling mediaeval symbols without dealing a serious blow to anyone. Rather, his strength comes from his faith, humility and authenticity. By discarding the trappings of residence and entourage, the Bishop of Rome reminds one of Jesus Christ starting out on his public ministry. There is something refreshing, authentic and challenging about the man 'from the ends of the earth' who says he wants to see a 'poor church, of the poor'. Christ himself began his public ministry saying that he came to bring good news to the poor and to set prisoners free. The Pope just celebrated Holy Thursday by washing the feet of 12 young inmates in a detention centre in his diocese. Here is a man of his time, not trying to live in the past or revive what has long passed. His church of the poor, however, must go beyond just giving food and shelter to the poverty stricken – itself essential – but ask why there are still 1.6 billion people living in penury. Helder Camara, former bishop of Recife in Brazil once said: "When I give food to the hungry, I am called a saint, when I ask why the poor have no food, they call me a communist." That is why the great challenge for Pope Francis I is not only to endorse charity but revive the social justice agenda. The past two pontiffs did everything possible to undermine liberation theology and punish, silence and harass its principal proponents. The purge took international dimension with demotion and side-lining of every possible threat even in the remotest corners of the church. The Kenyan Church is also a part of this reductionism in the social justice agenda and intolerance of prophetic voices for social justice. The Church provides a wide range of services to the marginalised but has no radical, innovative or creative agenda to address great inequalities in our society. There is also a cosy, working relationship with the ruling class that prevents any challenge to the status quo, most recently seen in early endorsement by some prelates of politicians even before they had been sworn in. Yet, the suggestion from the Pope that he will launch the process of the beatification of Oscar Romero of El Salvador does represent a radical shift in Vatican thinking and gives hope that the 'poor might inherit the earth'.

IDPs should emulate Muteshi's courage
(July 13 2013)

Adrian Muteshi's determination to repossess his 100-acre farm in Turbo is both inspiring and daring. He and his family must have experienced many doubts, threats and questions during the five-year court battle in Eldoret. Earlier in the hearing, he declined to accept an out-of-court settlement since there was no guarantee of it including compensation and court expenses. He remained focused and unyielding right up to the final court ruling. Mr Muteshi expressed reservations about the Sh5 million compensation for the loss of harvest he incurred for five years. The figure appears inadequate and disproportionate to his loss of income, but his decision not to contest it will mean that he can go ahead and return to his home just as soon as Mr Ruto removes his property and livestock. Mr Ruto has announced his decision to contest the judgment. Should he pursue that line, then he will be obliged to testify since in the recently concluded case, he chose not to defend himself. Of course, the Deputy President may have been innocently misled into acquiring Mr Muteshi's property. Many have lauded the court decision as a further sign of the new independence in the Judiciary, but wondered why Mr Ruto was deemed to have merely trespassed on Mr Muteshi's property. It appeared more like an invasion and dispossession. Indeed, it is hardly credible that the Deputy President was not aware of the circumstances in which Mr Muteshi was removed from his own shamba. Of course, many further questions will now arise regarding Chapter Six of the Constitution on Integrity and Leadership and the ICC will also be keeping a close eye on events as they unfold. However, beyond this, the Muteshi case raises many questions about property owners in the Rift Valley and elsewhere who are in a similar predicament. There are hundreds of property owners who were evicted in the post-election violence of 2007-8 and whose land is occupied by others until today. Many IDPs may have been resettled elsewhere, but the desire and entitlement to return to your own home remains. Both Mr Ruto and Mr Kenyatta promised that the Jubilee coalition would reconcile the Kikuyu and Kalenjin communities. They must now prove that this goes beyond them and that reconciliation includes returning peacefully to your own property. Some faith-based initiatives [that] have done exemplary work in this respect. But there are thousands of families still living as displaced and bitter persons all over the country. Despite public perception that it was mainly Kikuyu who were displaced, the truth is that many Kalenjin, Kisii and Luhyas were also evicted from Nakuru, Uasin Gishu, Trans Nzoia and Kericho counties. Mr Ruto's name is severely tarnished over the Muteshi case. Yet if he were to launch genuine reconciliation in his own backyard by welcoming back displaced people, then his offence would quickly be absolved. Mr Muteshi has shown exemplary courage and determination, but it should not be necessary for each victim to resort to the court to acquire justice.

Would our annual prayers impress Christ?
(July 20 2013)

A few weeks back, we had the annual national prayer breakfast which was broadcast live for those not fortunate enough to be invited. Most of Jesus' teachings were delivered at table settings and many of his parables focused on weddings, banquets and meals. Meals and fellowship are part of Christian life, but would Christ be impressed by our national prayers and sumptuous feasting? Different churches have different traditions but Christ spent most of his time sharing food and drink with outcasts, women and the sick. He ate with sinners, hung out with prostitutes and invited the poor to meals. Indeed, his most memorable miracles were reserved for the hungry who stayed with him till late when kiosks were closed. Were he to be invited to our annual prayer breakfast, I guess Jesus would show up with friends from Korogocho, Mandera or Bangla, and would insist that they occupy the low places but end up eating the most? He would not miss a chance to challenge politicians, priests and the press about their lavishness and would question the elitism of the guest list. His mission, quite simply, was to comfort the afflicted and to afflict the comfortable. There is no intention here to condemn organisers of these events as our country needs prayers. However, when they are conducted in their current state, they promote the prosperity gospel rather than the message of liberation Jesus taught. Much of the contemporary Christian preaching promotes a simplistic message that salvation will lead to wealth and prosperity. When preachers travel in jets, live in luxury and ask you to send prayer requests by M-Pesa, then that heresy is reinforced. Prayer breakfasts conveniently avoid inviting or dwelling on the poor, hungry or marginalised. Shameless and greedy legislators see no dichotomy in praising God and worshipping wealth. Religion that focuses on escaping from reality rather than engaging in the murky reality of our public life is another form of addiction. Even mainstream churches have lost their voice as both CJPC and NCCK have been tamed, silenced and side-lined by religious autocrats. The Jubilee government has neither opposition in Parliament nor out of it. It would appear very hopeless if it were not for the single voice of the man from down under, Pope Francis I who attempts to bring morality, sanity and the voice of the poor back to the Catholic Church. Last week he went to the island of Lampedusa to lay a wreath and bring focus to the 19,000 Africans who have drowned seeking a better life in Europe. He did not protest when a Curia official was arrested for money laundering and has made great strides in appointing a collegial council to govern and reform the Church. Will the Church in Kenya follow his example of justice and simplicity?

If Pope doesn't judge gays, how can we?
(August 17 2013)

Pope Francis has captured the world's imagination by his informal style of manners and speech. He seems to have an innate ability to speak directly to the heart of the common person even when dealing with the most difficult of topics. Two weeks ago, he gave a press conference during his flight back to Rome from World Youth Celebrations in Brazil and candidly answered questions on a variety of subjects including the thorny issue of homosexuality. "Who am I to judge if someone is gay and searches for the Lord and has good will?" he stated. His audience must have been dumbfounded by this response and may have wished to retort "you are the Pope, and we expect you to have all the answers". The Pontiff not only showed humility in his response but also respect by referring to gays as 'gays' the term in which they prefer to be recognised. Many refer to gays as homosexuals or speak of the 'homosexual condition' as if it were a medical condition or worse still an illness. But Francis chose not to go down that dismissive or judgmental path and added "gays should not be marginalised because of their orientation but they must be integrated into society. The problem is not having this orientation. We must be brothers and sisters." In a most radical way, he was saying that gays do not choose gayism as a lifestyle or as a deviant behaviour. Rather it is their innate orientation. That was ground-breaking teaching even if it might have left many of the Catholic faithful confused and even angry. In one swift statement, he was calling a halt to all discrimination, hatred and prejudice by taking one small but very significant step towards reversing centuries of dehumanisation of gay people. By accepting the existence of gay people and by referring to them as brothers and sisters, the Pope removed any legitimacy for judging and condemning them. By honouring gay people, the Pontiff could not be so naïve as to suggest that gay love should not be expressed. Yet, 'homosexual acts' are illegal in 38 countries worldwide, including Kenya. When President Barack Obama visited Africa recently, he called for respect, equality and recognition of the gay community and for the repeal of the criminalisation of homosexual acts. His comments met a hostile reception in the continent and locally, with John Cardinal Njue claiming "we need to act according to our own traditions and our faiths and these people who have already ruined their society let them not become our teachers to tell us where to go." That opinion is fairly representative of the prejudices that portray gayism as a foreign import that will destroy African cultures and faiths. Yet, the Pope says it is an orientation and as such is found everywhere. We may find it abhorrent, disgusting or sinful but gays are our brothers and sisters, and who are we to judge them? They clearly have not selected their orientation any more than the rest of us have chosen to be attracted to the opposite sex. That may be a hard pill to swallow but it is what the Pontiff said.

Loyalists, artists awarded for a reason
(December 14 2013)

Tomorrow, Madiba will be laid to rest in Qunu. The earth will tremble as it embraces a great leader while the heavens will rock with the entry of a soul adored by billions. Madiba will be welcomed home by Albert Luthuli, Joe Slovo, Ruth First, Walter Sisulu, Miriam Makeba, Chris Hani and other compatriots. Only one anti-apartheid struggle hero remains: Desmond Tutu. What a collection of extraordinary selfless, courageous and inspiring people! History has taught us that the greater the persecution and injustice, the greater the quality of leaders who rise up and oppose it. South Africa has produced a greater number of heroes and heroines in the past

50 years than any other country on the planet. Recently, I spotted a list of Kenyans nominated for awards and honours as part of the Kenya at 50 celebrations. They were a fairly motley bunch of civil servants and loyalists. An earlier list was headed by Inspector-General of Police David Kimaiyo who has done nothing since his appointment to make the country safer. The public was requested to give comments on the nominees' suitability, but most Kenyans wouldn't bother to reply and even if they took time, would most probably say 'none of the above please'. Yet, such lists are very telling about the ruling elite's priorities, loyalties and values. Those selected confirm that Kenya ina wenyewe and the past 50 years have mostly been about them, their comfort, perks, grabbed land and their very lopsided perception of patriotism. There is no interest in honouring Mama Koigi or Wanjiku; no place of honour for Nyayo torture survivors; no posthumous awards for [Pio Gama Pinto], JM Kariuki, Tom Mboya, Alexander Muge or John Kaiser. Threats and insults are what today's heroes, like George Kegoro, Njonjo Mue and Gladwell Otieno, who dared to defend victims' rights recently at the ICC, receive. Sports stars, religious leaders and artists, who pose no threat to the status quo, will be honoured, but critics, investigative journalists or human rights defenders must rely on prayers of the marginalised for encouragement. The beneficiaries of Thursday's awards are mere actors and tools in the official historical script that the establishment would like Kenyans to adopt. But there are other narratives and brave stories not heard. The poor who have endured corruption, greed, poverty, hardship and political violence for half a century were omitted from the establishment's narrative. But they, too, have produced mothers and children, whose names are surely written in heaven alongside Madiba even if they never made the Kenya Gazette. Their heroism and faith have kept Kenya sane, progressive and bravely resisting repressive regimes. The next 50 years belong to them. We can no longer afford to side-line, bulldoze, enslave, bully or intimidate the 60 per cent, who only create joy out of scraps that fall from the decadent ruling class's table. A radical transformation of society begins with a fundamental option to hear the narrative of the poor.

Bishops wrong on anti-tetanus drive
(April 5 2014)

Two weeks ago, I met a team of Community Health Workers (CHWs) as they launched their door-to-door Neonatal Tetanus Campaign. Ours was one of 60 districts in 16 counties targeted for the second phase of the exercise. These women explained how Kenya was one of 51 countries globally with high rates of tetanus infection passed between mother and infant at childbirth. In fact, Kenya had 555 cases last year; and 110,000 deaths occur annually as a result of tetanus infection in children. By immunising the mother, the mother passes on immunity to her infant and so we are able to radically reduce infant mortality rates. Three days later one of the team came dashing into my office in a state of panic. "What are we to do now that Cardinal Njue has said that the vaccine will make us all infertile? Whom do we believe — the Government or the Church?' she raged. I was flabbergasted as this was the first I had heard of Cardinal Njue's concerns. Give me time, I pleaded. I quickly discovered that the cardinal had asked why only women were vaccinated; why there was so little collaboration with the churches and such poor awareness about the matter in the country. But the Health Commission of the Bishops Conference went further and claimed that in similar campaigns in Nicaragua, Mexico and the Philippines, the vaccine was laced with a hormone that left women permanently infertile. While not directly accusing the Ministry of Health, they stated that they were 'not certain that the vaccines being used in Kenya are free of this hormone'. Suspicion had been planted. Cabinet Secretary James Macharia then announced on March 26 that he had met the cardinal and that the issue had been resolved. But four days later the bishops bought space in the Sunday press to repeat their claims and demands. And there the matter ended inconclusively. The bishops have so far not produced any evidence that the vaccine was a birth control method, but two million women targeted in the exercise deserve an explanation. I have met women who are worried and angry about the bishops intervention. Others responded to the scare by boycotting the vaccination and in the process may have endangered their health. The bishops have a moral duty to produce the evidence or apologise to women and Ministry of Health. Medical and scientific experts say that there is no way you can sterilise a woman in this manner, and despite experiments 20 years ago, the medical world has so far not developed a birth control vaccine. It is sad that bishops put [their] energy into an area that they have least expertise and experience in — sexuality — and say nothing about insecurity, corruption, laptops and access to health services. Last September Pope Francis said that the church cannot always be obsessed with issues of abortion, sexuality, family planning: "We have to find a new balance otherwise the moral edifice of the church will collapse like a house of cards, losing the freshness and fragrance of the Gospel." Did our bishops read his 'Joy of the Gospel'?

The Bishop with the fifty-bob legacy
(April 19 2014)

On Tuesday, Mombasa may well come to a halt as the church and public say farewell to retired Archbishop Boniface Lele who passed away 10 days ago. Yet the simple, gentle soul from rural Kitui would most probably be embarrassed by all the attention and speeches. Boniface was a rarity among public figures: humble, approachable, gentle, unpretentious and very uncomfortable with all the trimmings and trappings of his position. Born into poverty, he died a poor man too: no overseas accounts, no profit-making plazas, no property that his family will quarrel over. When my colleague Nicky browsed his wallet for his ID to acquire a burial permit, he found a mere fifty-bob note, his total legacy. That was typical of a man who would dispatch his monthly stipend by M-Pesa in five minutes. There were always pressing needs: hospital bills, school fees, seeds for planting. He was generous to a fault as he would often remain with nothing to pay his own bills. He had the 'Francis effect' before anyone knew about the man from Argentina. He was a shepherd that 'smelled of the sheep' long before the Pope exhorted his colleagues to do so. Friend in word and deed his mercy firstly extended to women and children and was best illustrated when he became the first and only Catholic bishop to advocate condom use for discordant couples to avoid infecting each other with HIV. He withstood the criticism and was very supportive when I revisited this important issue in this column three years ago. He will also be remembered for informing ICC indictees Uhuru Kenyatta and William Ruto in 2011 that their prayer crusade would not be welcome in any Catholic Church in the coastal region. He spoke openly about his own illness that forced him to retire early after being diagnosed with dementia. He did not demand special care but chose to move to Changamwe where he bore his illness without complaint, in the company of friends and the occasional malt beer! Boniface Lele was no saint but when you peruse the passion narratives of the man from Nazareth you find a lot of similarities. Nothing quite moves us like authenticity. Jesus too was stripped of friends and clothing as he died humiliated and naked on the cross. We have been covering up his nakedness and concealing his humanity ever since as preachers present a plastic Jesus that guarantees you prosperity in this life and salvation in the next, provided you top up their M-Pesa account every Sunday from the comfort of your armchair. The prosperity and glitzy gospel seem far removed from the man crucified among thieves in Golgotha. Being truly human is not about gathering possessions but rather letting go of illusions, attachments, embracing people and the truth and being willing to suffer and die for what is right and true. It is about being faithful to your conscience. It is also walking gently on the earth, leaving small footprints for that is what humility really is. That and the fifty-bob note is Boniface Lele's enduring legacy to the people of Mombasa and Kitui. May he rest in peace and rise at Easter.

PSC is overseeing negative ethnicity
(January 17 2015)

Skewed distribution of national resources, appointments and public service jobs are the critical issues that divide this nation and maintain the scourge that is negative ethnicity. The Constitution was designed to promote equal access to resources and opportunities and to give every community a sense of participation and sharing in the life of the nation. Devolution has gone some way towards the redistribution of the nation's wealth but does the public service adequately represent the face of Kenya and what measures have the Public Service Commission (PSC) taken to bring equity in appointment in line with the national values? These are the questions that Chair Margaret Kobia tried to address in her December report on PSC's progress on compliance with Articles 10 and 232 of the Constitution. The lengthy report covers many aspects of compliance but most attention understandably has been focused on the Ethnic Audit aspect of its contents. PSC reports that the Kalenjin, Kikuyu, Kisii and Embu communities are over-represented in the public service while Somali, Turkana and Maasai are severely underrepresented. In figures this means that while Kikuyu make up 17.33 per cent of the population, they hold 22.87 per cent of the jobs while Kalenjin have 12.81 per cent of the jobs and are 11.24 per cent of the population. Put another way, Kikuyu have 31 per cent more jobs than they should and Kalenjin have an additional 14 per cent. At the other end Somalis are 6.25 per cent of population, but only hold 1.85 per cent of PSC positions. In other words, they only get 30 per cent of their quota. The Turkana are even worse off, having only 0.4 per cent or 384 of the 94,286 jobs despite being 2.59 per cent of the population, a mere 15 per cent of their representation. The PSC inherited most of those imbalances but states that "new appointments in 2013/14 reflect a fairer progression in ethnic balancing in the public service" (Pg. 67). However, when you go to the appendices you discover that the opposite is true. A massive 83 per cent of the jobs available in that period went the way of the Luo, Kikuyu, Kalenjin and Luhya communities, yet they make up only 54 per cent of the population. Throw in the Kamba and you discover that the big five got 91 per cent of the jobs despite making up only 64 per cent of the population. The biggest beneficiaries were the Kalenjin who got 22.58 per cent of jobs, but are only 11.24 per cent of population and the Luo who got 19 per cent of jobs but are only 10.58 per cent of population. Both communities got nearly twice as many jobs as they should have. This is a shocking indictment of PSC's failure in compliance of "representation of Kenya's diverse ethnic communities" (Article 232). What does the Commission for the Implementation of the Constitution have to say about this abuse? How can Prof Kobia defend such blatant discrimination and contempt for the Constitution? What measures are the CIC and NCIC taking in public universities where in 2012, 80 per cent of Bondo University staff were Luo, 83 per cent of Meru were locals and 71 per cent of Pwani University staff were Mijikenda? Statistics if available for ethnic audits in the counties would probably be even damning but PSC has been condemned by its very own report and its appendices.

Where can we find humble leaders?
(March 7 2015)

Should President Kenyatta approve the new laws passed by Parliament last week, then we may well be spared the screaming sirens and 'Your Excellency' salutations that have accompanied the 47 governors for the past two years. It seems that as soon as politicians start climbing the ladder, they suddenly become king, consistently reminding us of their new powers, while conveniently forgetting the oaths of service they took. It is, of course, not just politicians who abuse power and the public, but most people who seem to be better off than the rest. A recent research in Europe showed that folks who drive SUVs are 50 per cent more likely to jump pedestrian crossings than those who drive smaller vehicles. Believe it or not, shoplifters are much more likely to be the rich than the down and out, as you might expect. There is something seductive about power, money and privilege that makes most believe that they are now above the law. Jesus himself spent his life resisting temptations to use his powers to be popular and wealthy. Somehow, the rich imagine that the law was designed to contain the poor, but they themselves have no need of observing those same laws. So, when we see the rich and political classes misbehave arrogantly and irreverently, we often think that is the same behaviour that got them up the rungs of the ladder in the first place. Not true, however. Most people were initially elected to office because they seemed to have a compassionate heart and a genuine desire to improve the lives of the poor. We all know people who worked alongside us with diligence and passion, but when they donned the suits and were granted security guards, they became nasty, arrogant individuals. Soon Uruguay will say goodbye to President Jose Mujica, regarded as the world's most humble leader. The 79-yearold drove around in a 1987 VW Beetle regularly giving hitchhikers a ride. He lived on his farm with his three-legged dog Manuela protected only by two policemen. History had taught him humility for he was shot six times and spent 14 years as a political prisoner. So, he gave away 90 per cent of his salary because he didn't need it and his real legacy will be the stable economy he leaves behind. For Mujica, to be humble is to be normal, decent and human; nothing special, no tricks, no PR — just authenticity. But how rare it is to find authentic individuals! Of course, to be humble is also a discipline, a habit, a choice of lifestyle that needs constant evaluation. Because our public culture is so flawed, we need advisors and laws that limit all of us. Whether we are politicians, cardinals, bankers or consultants we need checks and balances that remind us of our primal duty to be accountable and serve. No quality is as admirable as humility among the powerful. This reminds one of the advice of the American activist Marian Wright Edelman: Service is the rent we pay for being, it is the very purpose of life, and not something we do in our spare time.

Coast fishermen have nowhere to land (March 14 2015)

Last month I visited my local butcher's to purchase some fish. No fresh fillet was available but I was offered frozen fish instead which I purchased at Sh500 per kilo. However, when I got home and examined the packaging, I discovered that while the fish was filleted and packaged in Mombasa, it had originated from Vietnam. Yes, Mombasa businesses are transporting fish from 8,000kms away while the local fishing industry is in rapid decline. It may sound incredible but the coast fishing industry produces only five percent of the 174,000 metric tonnes of fish produced in Kenya each year. That is a shocking statistic as lack of modernisation, the absence of investment and, in particular, corruption has led to the collapse of a traditionally key local industry. My colleagues at Haki Yetu have spent months researching and documenting the plight of the small scale or artisan fishermen in Mombasa County. In the soon-to-be released report appropriately entitled 'Nowhere to Land,' they reveal how poor fishermen lose their landing sites on a regular basis to land

and beach grabbers in the coastal county. There are 14 gazetted landing sites in Mombasa and 36 more traditionally used by the fishermen for decades. However, not even the gazetted ones have proper documentation or title deeds and so industries, government parastatals, hoteliers and greedy opportunists have encroached upon the landing sites and evicted the poor fisher folk. Today fishermen are only able to access less than 40 percent of their landing sites [which] are gradually being replaced by hotels, private mansions, bridges and industrial sites. The fishing industry in Mombasa also suffers like many other sectors in the agricultural area, with low budgets and poor investment. Fishermen live a hand-to-mouth existence forced to sell off their produce cheaply each day due to lack of stores and freezers. The only cold storage facilities in Mombasa are in Old Town and they are constantly under repair. Fisheries have become devolved but that has made little difference in approach or support. In its first budget for the year 2013/14 the county government budgeted Sh350 million for the purchase of 10 motorboats for the various Beach Management Units (BMUs) but in budget cuts they were among the first projects to be abandoned. So, while the Kenya coast has a 350 nautical mile of an Exclusive Economic Zone (EEZ) that protects its fishing rights, the artisans are unable to take advantage. Worse still European and Asian trawlers consistently fish in Kenyan waters because of poor supervision by the fisheries department. It makes depressing reading as the children of humble, hardworking and impoverished fisherman no longer feel they have a future in an industry that has been family based for generations. Sadly, the same story could be repeated about the plight of the maize farmers in the Rift Valley and the sugarcane workers in Western. Corruption, greed and negligence are killing food industries and destroying lives and livelihoods. So, we end up allowing cheaper imported sugar, maize and now fish drive Kenyan workers onto the unemployment line and do nothing to protect and promote our own food chain.

Nkaissery must end Turkana-Pokot war (March 28 2015)

Kainuk in South Turkana is back in the news for all the wrong reasons. Photos in mainstream and social media of residents demonstrating that 'Tumechoka kuzika' (we are tired burying) would bring tears to any eye. Yes, the village of 300 graves and as many widows is telling the nation that they, too, have a Right to Life. But is anyone listening? Fifteen years ago, colleagues and I closed the main KitaleLodwar road in the border village for the first time to highlight the vulnerability of the

Turkana community. While the area then experienced reduction in loss of life for a decade, the resumption of the slaughter since the discovery of oil and the coming to power of the Jubilee administration has reached dangerous levels. Not just in Kainuk, but Lorogon, Nakwamoru and 200 kilometres away in Kapedo, Turkanas appear to be under siege from their Pokot neighbours in a manner that cannot be dismissed as traditional cattle rustling. What is going on appears more like planned expansionism together with utter lawlessness to which the interior security ministry has chosen to turn a blind eye. The area around the Turkwell Gorge has been contested ever since the power plant, one of Kenya's first mega corruption deals, was constructed nearly three decades ago. The Kanu solution to the contested territory was to appoint chiefs in both counties as administrators of the same location. Working with both communities, however, we managed to temporarily transform the conflict by campaigning for both the Pokot and Turkana to access power as initially all electricity generated at the gorge was transferred directly to the national grid 200 kilometres away. That brought change but not resolution, and today, the area is a war zone. This week, two Pokot Police Reserves were gunned down and vehicles carrying water to Turkana burnt to cinders. That led to more protests in Kapenguria, as the Pokot mourned their slain children. A few months ago, 21 police officers were gunned down in Kapedo in a confessed "mistaken" identity slaughter that had no repercussions. This week, the county government of Turkana has gone to court to demand that the national government address the boundaries and insecurity issue. Thankfully, they are turning to the force of law rather than the law of force. But can the Judiciary grant a win-win verdict? Something more inclusive is required to compliment the legal approach. Cabinet Secretary Nkaissery must wake up, too, and flex his muscles. Criminals on either side need to be treated accordingly, but neither community needs to be criminalised or victimised if cohesion is the goal. Talk of repairing the Kitale-Lokichoggio road has just remained at that noisy level. Both communities would benefit from decent access to Sudan, where Pokots could sell their cement, and Turkanas find opportunities denied to them at home. Both communities have far more in common than they would dare to admit. But both counties have elected representatives that have no idea of what democracy entails. Other voices need to be heard, who will expose the warlords and bring sanity and harmony back to the vast area.

Focus on Shabaab, NGOs are innocent
(June 6 2015)

I am more frequently found on the other side of the confessional box but now it's my turn to humbly beat my breast. Two years ago, I attended a series of secret meetings with the Mombasa Republic Council (MRC). The gatherings were convened by the National Cohesion and Integration Commission (NCIC) for the purpose of dialoguing with the secessionist group. Our motives were genuine but according to Fazul Mahamed, executive director of the NGOs Co-ordination Board, any engagement with the outlawed MRC is an illegal act. That is one of several reasons Muhuri is under the spotlight from the board. Mr Mahamed also has grave reservations about the human rights body's failure to notify him that Maina Kiai, Sarah Kinyanjui and I joined the board without being vetted by the Government oversight and management body. He says "the unprocedural change of officials points to a mischievous and calculated move to evade vetting of the officials". No room for an administrative oversight error there. The board chief sees calculated mischief in our appointment and we should expect a thorough vetting before ever being approved. Mr Mahamed also has issues with Muhuri opening bank accounts and employing foreigners — not me, I hope, since my services are all [voluntary]— without his approval. Makes you wonder what is going on at the NGO body as those are allegations which Muhuri has to respond to within 14 days or legal action will follow. I noted a sense of glee in Fazul's eyes as he told the cameras that Haki Africa would be hauled off to court for operating under another organisation's registration. Anyone with a passing knowledge of the NGO world will tell you that the Independent Medico Legal Unit (IMLU) functioned for over a decade under the banner of the Bungoma Professionals Association when they were denied registration [by] the Moi regime. The NGOs board is the latest government entity enlisted to investigate, intimidate and preoccupy the two civil society organisations. Earlier it was the CID, NIS and the KRA, with the cooperation of junior magistrates. Of course, it needs to be pointed out that Muhuri has not been deregistered. The source of that hoax carried in the *Nation* seems to be a State House blogger who appears to have more influence and contacts than one would expect from a man who is just qualified for tweeting. However, the whole episode does reveal the Executive's preoccupation with clamping down on civil society rather than concentrating on fighting Al-Shabaab. That the focus for the intimidation is Muslim based organisations will only give further proof that the Muslim community as a whole has been profiled and is under suspicion. Named politicians with an expansionist agenda together with funders of cattle rustling in the North Rift drift in and out of State

House on a daily basis and mingle with high profile land grabbers and beneficiaries of grand corruption. But the Muslim community has been found guilty until proven innocent; and that is most manifest in the harassment of Muhuri and Haki Africa. It does not augur well for the nation's cohesion nor does it make Kenya any safer.

The cry of the earth is the cry of the poor
(June 27 2015)

The announcement that Pope Francis will visit Kenya in November was received with excitement not only by Catholics but by all people of goodwill. What marks this pontiff apart is his broad appeal to every faith and nation, thanks to his ordinariness, inclusivity, mercy and challenging good sense. Last week he released an encyclical on the environment and ecology — Laudato Si — that was addressed to the whole of humanity. Pope Francis was not just bringing the Catholic voice to the environmental table but giving a critique and moral solution to the whole human family on the issue of environmental destruction. He boldly stated that human activity is the principal cause of climate change and destruction of the planet and that greed taking precedence over need has put our very existence at risk. The encyclical states emphatically that the poor have their needs denied while the rich have their appetites indulged. Indeed, the poor world pays the biggest price for the harm inflicted on the planet by the self-indulgence of the rich. The poor are the first hit by climate disasters through floods, heatwaves, droughts and crop failure. The pope is presenting a moral solution to a moral problem and at the same time is critiquing capitalism. The market does not care about the common good or the long-term survival of the planet. Its concern is profit and choice but the pontiff warns, "Our freedom fades when it is handed over to the blind forces of the unconscious, of immediate needs, of self-interest and violence." Economics based on unlimited growth cannot continue so the rich must radically change and learn to be satisfied with less. Our "collective selfishness" meets short-term wants rather than our long-term needs. At the moment we are turning the planet into a giant dustbin with our disposable culture where we use and dump commodities and even each other. Temporary solutions like recycling are not enough and there is no technological fix either. The pope is emphatic that "we must integrate questions of justice in the debate on the environment, so as to hear both the cry of the earth and the cry of the poor." Put another way, humanity is reminded how our relationships with the earth and the poor have become distorted and imbalanced and are now putting our future in peril. The care of the earth and care of the poor are inextricably linked.

147

What legacy are we giving our grandchildren? What climatic disasters await the planet from human activity and its selfishness? Developed countries have used up more than their fair share of the earth's resources and are now morally obliged to compensate poorer countries — like Kenya — in what the pontiff calls "ecological debt". The clear message is that we are sleepwalking into disaster, but is anyone listening? But do we have a choice as we cannot go on living as we are. Simple technological solutions will not avert the imminent catastrophe either. This document for all humanity most certainly will discover its local context when the pope comes visiting in November.

Regret by Britain over torture not enough
(September 12 2015)

We live in a time of global apologies. Nations, faiths and leaders of every description are apologising to former enemies, minorities, victims, prisoners, children and women. We have developed a new language of closure, reconciliation, acknowledgment, reparations and restitution. The world seems determined to never again repeat the horrific crimes of the past and to move towards a new era of accountability and respect for the rule of law. This mood for closure seems to have gripped Kenya or at least the former [colonial] masters, the British. In June 2013, the British Government reached an out-of-court settlement with the Mau Mau veterans, who had taken a case on behalf of the victims of torture and ill-treatment [during 1952-63 in the colonial era]. As a result, the British Government, through Mau Mau advocates Leigh Day, has paid out Sh340,000 to each of 5,228 victims. A second part of the settlement followed when Foreign Secretary William Hague issued a statement of regret for those dreadful colonial crimes. The third and final piece of the agreement will take place today at Freedom Corner, Nairobi, when a monument will be unveiled to the heroes and heroines of the colonial repression. I expect that the British High Commissioner will speak of closure while Kenya will respond by accepting the settlement terms. Does the matter end there? Is this reconciliation? Whatever has been achieved to date must be attributed solely to the sterling efforts of the Kenya Human Rights Commission, who started the process by honouring and documenting the cases of the victims. They also funded investigations and litigation until the case was given over to Leigh Day. Successive governments have paid lip service to the cause though today they will want to receive the plaudits. Today's event, however, is highly significant because the British Government is finally acknowledging its misdeeds. Acknowledgment means officially sanctioning what

Kenyans already know that during the Emergency, up to 30,000 Kenyans were eliminated by state forces, while 32 Europeans were killed by the Mau Mau; half-a-million were detained in camps and enclosed villages and over 1,000 convicted political prisoners were sent to the gallows. So, is a mere 'regret' adequate to address that level of torture and tyranny? Does it not appear like a half-hearted apology and insincere conclusion to what many consider genocide? Today, I hope that the British Government will tell Kenyans that they are 'sorry' and admit that they are 'guilty' of crimes against humanity; that they sincerely apologise and signs of repentance are visible. Beyond erecting a monument at Freedom Corner, there is also a need to erect another one at Trafalgar Square or Downing Street to commemorate the victims of torture and ill-treatment in Kenya. Monuments are there to remind us of the past, not just the glorious but even the inglorious moments and events that we would want to forget. Kenyans know their history, but the British need not only to acknowledge Waterloo and Dunkirk, but also be educated on the shocking crimes committed by the imperial empire. That monument in London might, indeed, symbolise a form of reconciliation that is genuine, inclusive and lasting.

Politics is the last refuge of a scoundrel
(December 12 2015)

It's holiday time but peak season for politicians masquerading as philanthropists, saviours, bull fighters, football referees and conveners of goat auctions. Campaigning will begin as soon as Christmas is over as the ballot is 'next year' — August 8, 2017 to be exact. The incumbents will be joined by the recycled, the neophytes, the bizarre and the exhibitionists, all wanting a piece of the action and a huge chunk of the cake. Judging by the calibre emerging, we should not expect anything [to] change. Once candidates don the 10-gallon hats, acquire an idler to carry their phone and christen him PA, dab their names on a public wall, they are in business. It is easy to be cynical about politicians. George Bernard Shaw said "politics is the last resort for the scoundrel". Were he alive in Kenya today, he might agree that politics is often the first refuge for the scoundrel, thief and idler? This 11th Parliament in Kenya is probably the most disgraced, incompetent and dishonest one of the lot. No wonder legislators are trying to secure pensions and medical allowances for themselves after just one term in office. They clearly know that up to 90 per cent of them will be sent home in 20 months and they dread the prospect of living out a life of ignominy, poverty and indifference. Of course, Parliament has no monopoly on corruption or greed. MCAs have shown that lack of education is no barrier to profiteering, bribery, extortion and blackmail of their assemblies. Kenyans are mad about politics but don't trust politicians in the slightest. The recent Freedom House poll showed that the media and civil society organisations are trusted much more than elected representatives. There is, however, something horribly wrong about Kenya politics. It seems to corrupt the best of people and when a colleague or friend joins politics you feel they are doomed and damned. For the most part, politics puts an end to a career of service and hard work. Put another way, how many former politicians have returned to civilian life and been successful in business or as professionals? Most of them are incapable of holding down a proper job so after losing elections they hang around Harambee House, Parliament or wherever and [seek] positions on irrelevant parastatal boards [that] offer them allowances and travel away from the embarrassment of being a 'nobody' in the village. This week, Speaker Justin Muturi brought the National Assembly to an unprecedented level of shame after being bullied by MPs to reject a report on parliamentary corruption and waste that he requested and whose contents he had endorsed. Mr Muturi wasted more taxpayers' money buying space in the print media to claim that the EACC was "irresponsible, premature and unprofessional". Is he in turn attempting to bully the EACC into silence and the public into amnesia? Kenya desperately needs an alternative. If the choice is either Cord or Jubilee, most thinking citizens would say neither. This is the right moment to launch a third party and give Kenyans a real choice. There are thousands of capable, decent people of integrity who must put country before self and save politics from politicians.

Grabbers, filthy cities killing our children
(July 30 2016)

Tourist arrivals may be on the rise, but on first impressions many may wonder about the wisdom of choosing Mombasa for rest and relaxation. Kibarani may be the gateway to the island and ocean, but the choking smoke and filthy stench from the nearby dumpsite is dangerous, hazardous and probably poisonous. Yet it's what every arrival first encounters. For the past three years, Mombasa County Government has spent a fortune on hired trucks and dumpers, depositing garbage and most likely toxic waste in the ocean while levelling the site. But nothing has improved. Visitors pass a few more horribly filthy dumpsites before reaching their beach hotel, but residents of Kibarani are being poisoned daily. Children in St Francis School have extremely high rates of respiratory illnesses resulting from breathing polluted air every minute of their tender, young lives. Nema does not care and

Kenyans have long ago given up on this most useless of institutions established to safeguard their environment. That is Mombasa, but it could be any urban centre in Kenya. Think of Nairobi's Dandora dumpsite or the Kisumu ones. More than half of the world's population now resides in cities and more than 50 per cent of Kenyans live in urban centres. However, most are filthy, unhealthy, overcrowded and un-planned settlements. They are monuments to greed and corruption as every urban settlement and development plan is sacrificed on the altars of expediency and capitalism. It's profit before people. Kenyans, however, will eternally be grateful to Wangari Maathai for her green initiatives and for saving Uhuru Park. Now, Nairobi Senator Mike Mbuvi wants to convert the largest green, public area in the city into a bus park. Our politicians have no notion of the benefits of green cities. They should listen to Pope Francis, who says about urban squalor: "We were not meant to be deprived of physical contact with nature." Politicians cannot grasp the interconnect-edness between shared spaces and human behaviour. Green areas and shared public spaces greatly enhance the quality of life, produce safer neighbourhoods and improve the physical and mental health of everyone. No wonder teenagers turn to crime and radicalism if they have nowhere to play or meet. London has a population of eight million, but 40 per cent of the city is green space. There are 142 parks, covering 1,600 square kilometres. Turn any corner in the bustling city and you find beautiful parks, playgrounds, sports fields and recreational spaces. That commitment to the common good was the best aspect of colonialism, but their urban plans have long since been decimated. Where are the shared spaces in our urban centres? Even areas set aside for public use in new estates have been grabbed by 'developers'. The more democratic any society becomes the more pub-lic funds will be spent on shared spaces, healthy environments and public safety. Small improvements like providing footpaths, play areas or green parks must be commended and encouraged. However, very little of devolution funds have been spent in these sectors that can make cities more beautiful, attractive and safe. The battle for life on earth will be won or lost in cities. Right now, we are losing that fight and our people are dying prematurely.

Debate on women priests is long overdue
(August 20 2016)

Whenever I attend a priestly ordination, I utter a silent prayer that one day women may be given the opportunity of serving humanity as ordained ministers. It is painful, embarrassing and almost impossible to defend women's current exclusion. Jesus chose 12 men as his Apostles but women were the first to witness his resurrection and then were sent to share the good news with the whole world. Jesus did not choose any Gentiles as Apostles, but no race has ever been excluded from priesthood. It is hard to imagine then that Jesus would have barred half of the planet from priesthood merely on biological grounds. Put rather more crudely, the uterus would hardly be an obstacle to priesthood for Jesus the liberator. But for centuries the ordained ministries of deacon, priest and bishop have been reserved for men in the Catholic Church. In recent times, Popes John Paul and Benedict even forbade all debate on the ordination of women. But with the new, refreshing openness of Pope Francis, humble debate and soul searching are not just tolerated, but encouraged. Two weeks ago, Pope Francis surprised many by announcing that he was setting up a study commission comprising 12 members — six male and six females — to research the viability of diaconate for women. The team does not comprise bishops or bureaucrats but a group of scholars; that composition is also telling. The basis for the study is that in the early church women deacons were ordained by the laying on of hands just like men. So, proponents will now argue that if women were deacons in the past, then why not today? Of course, opponents will argue that deacons were not ordained and that it was just a ministry of service to the poor. However, it is generally accepted that sacramental orders have three levels: Deacons, priests and bishops. Saying that out loud is enough to get angry reaction from opponents to women's ordination. Pope Francis is very aware of the fear of causing schism in the church. However, he is taking a bold step, even if it's a small one. Women have offered enormous service to the world over the centuries, displaying courage, mercy, wisdom and leadership in education, health and social services. However, they have never been granted leadership and decision-making positions in the church. Their voice is on the margins and their opinions merely consultative. This, however, is not a rights issue; it's much bigger than that. It's not about dressing women in dog-collars and clerical garb. It is not imitation but complementarity. The Catholic Church has for centuries missed the charisms and gifts that women can bring to the table and altar. The creativity, colour, sensitivity and warmth that women possess are urgently needed in the church. One could argue that the whole sexual abuse of children scandal could have been avoided had women been in a leadership and oversight role in the Catholic Church. Pope Francis has brought energy, life and humility back to the church. Indeed, his leadership now permits me to write this piece without fearing the belt of an episcopal crozier. Let the debate begin and let it be robust.

Life needs protection from womb to tomb (December 3 2016)

Groucho Marx once said that there are two things that can't be avoided in life, paying taxes and death. Death is the great equaliser, yet we all make valiant efforts to postpone that critical moment. Families sell their last acres of land to acquire life-saving treatment for their loved ones while hospital negligence that causes avoidable deaths is now considered an outrageous scandal. The measure of any society is how it responds to avoidable deaths like hunger, negligence, road accidents and killings. Ultimately, the litmus test for the 2010 Constitution is how it protects and enhances human life. Improved services mean a better quality of life for everyone. But humanity often expresses inconsistencies in its respect and protection for human life. We condemn extra judicial killings but tolerate mob justice. We say everyone has a right to life but still retain the death penalty on the statute books. Every year, 57 million people die globally, but it is estimated that a similar number of abortions are procured annually. Somehow, abortion is not deemed an avoidable death. We spend huge amounts to ensure safe delivery of our children but turn a blind eye to those denied entry into the universe. The right to life should begin in the womb and end with the tomb, with every aspect of life in between protected, enhanced and secured. Yet, how sad to read in last week's Saturday Nation the story of 'Sarah' who, out of shame at the prospect of being an unwed mother, felt the only way out was to procure an abortion. She feared rejection by her family and church, and afterwards as she grieved over her decision and loss discovered that there was no forum in her faith community to listen, embrace and support her. We condemn women for abortions but fail to acknowledge that abortion is a society failure, starting with the father of the aborted baby. The *Nation* report also tells us that in 2012 up to 120,000 women were treated for unsafe abortions in this country. It is not enough, however, to promote the right of women to free, safe, quality family planning methods. We also need to ensure as a society that every child born into the universe will be welcomed unconditionally, regardless of the health of the baby or the status of the mother. In that way women are supported to carry their babies until delivery even if they never wanted to get pregnant. In any case, how many of us can honestly say that our parents planned our families. I imagine most of us were unplanned but welcomed and loved. Put another way, if a woman cannot meet all the challenges of motherhood then society must. Pope Francis recently announced that all priests will have the power to absolve the sin of abortion. He in the process extended his mission of mercy. However, mercy by churches and society must go beyond forgiveness. We must find ways to accommodate, support, embrace and welcome women who cannot cope with the responsibilities of parenthood. There must be space in churches for forgiveness but also healing, restoration and parental support. Only then can will the number of avoidable deaths reduce.

Terrorists don't really believe God is great (March 11 2017)

Terrorism has not just brought death, destruction and division to Kenya; it has also changed the way we work, recreate and even worship. Terror has also produced an opposing narrative or response that we now refer to as CVE or Countering Violent Extremism. The Government has its own national strategy on CVE and many counties have also crafted their own plans that include civil society and religious organisations as well as the state security machinery. This is a very encouraging move. Yet how much effort is made to change the minds of young people and to give them sound religious teaching and alternative non-violent methods to express their alienation in society? Whenever there is a religious terror attack in Berlin, Istanbul, Wajir or wherever, we are usually told that the suicide bomber or assassin shouted 'Allahu Akbar' (God is Great) as he committed his heinous act. Most consider such terrorists as religious fanatics. Truth, however, is that such people are only half-believers. They believe that they have to defend God and act on his behalf since he appears too weak to take care of his own interests. They imagine that God is under threat and that the world could become a godless one if they don't rid it of all profanities. Put another way, they suggest that God is not quite up to the task that he set for himself and they have to step in. Such is the blasphemy of the religious terrorist. They want to save God, forgetting of course that it is God who saves people. If the terrorist really believed that God is great, he would not kill in his name, for God is able to do his own work without any violent assistance from humanity. This has been the fundamentalist flaw in every religion over the centuries. This is the heresy that gave birth to the Crusades and it influences Al Shabaab and Isis today. We only half believe but that half can cause harm to our neighbour and to our planet. The Irish writers Jonathan Swift said three centuries ago that we have just enough religion to make us hate but not enough to make us love one another. Half belief and half-baked religion are a recipe for ignorance, violence and destruction. That is why we must incorporate religious leaders into CVE if we want a long-term solution to the terror threat. Secondly, civil society and religious organisations must rediscover the beauty and truthfulness of Active Non-Violence (ANV) as preached and practised by Martin Luther King and Mahatma Gandhi. Gandhi taught that non-violence is the weapon of the strong who resist evil and organise citizens to overcome tyranny, poverty and injustice. MLK adopted his teaching saying that ANV is not a method for cowards as it encourages resistance, organised resistance. It is the only method that can bring about positive change without you getting killed in the process. Pope Francis says non-violence is a style of politics for peace — not passivity but active engagement. Eventually good theological and non-violent teaching alone will change minds, hearts and systems and bring about the change that Kenyan youth yearn for.

Society still applauds extra judicial killings (July 1 2017)

A year has passed since Willie Kimani, Josephat Mwenda and Joseph Muiruri were brutally assassinated by Kenyan police. The extra-judicial killing of the young lawyer and his two colleagues provoked national outrage. We prayed, protested and warned that 'never again' would such contempt for the rule of law be tolerated. We got angry but privately knew that we faced an uphill battle in the fight against summary executions. A few weeks ago, Mombasa police entered Kisauni in search of four young men reported to be members of a criminal gang. They were dragged from their hideouts, summarily executed and buried within twenty-four hours because their Muslim parents didn't want a post-mortem. This was a minor news item for half a day as media houses currently prefer to headline campaign circuses. Police killings are so common and acceptable that they no longer make news. The Independent Medico Legal Unit (IMLU) recently reported that 74 Kenyans died from police bullets in the first four months of 2017. The actual figures are probably much higher but who cares? Most Kenyans applaud such trigger-happy policemen in the mistaken belief that such killings are a sign that they are winning the war on crime. The political class play along with the police propaganda that criminals deserve to die and communities are much safer thanks to the police actions. The common denominator among most victims of police killings is that they were poor. They may have been involved in petty crime or gang activities so most believe they deserved to die because they were an immediate and visible threat to our safety. That is the strange logic that justifies, excuses and approves such contempt for due process. What if we applied the same thinking to the not so poor in our society? What if police were encouraged to execute politicians who steal land from schools or IDPs? What about the architects of Anglo Leasing, Goldenberg, Chickengate, Eurobond? Should the police not be permitted to eliminate them too since the courts have failed so miserably to provide restorative or retributive justice? Provocative questions indeed but in our warped thinking and crippled criminal justice system, due process is denied to the poor but mostly shields the privileged from accountability and punishment. At last week's memorial service for Willie Kimani and his colleagues, Njonjo Mue accused the church of 'largely remaining eloquent in its silence, conspicuous in its absence and distinguished in its indifference' to extra-judicial killings. Harsh words but how often have religious leaders joined the protests or issued pastoral letters on extra-judicial killings? The only voices of outrage come from civil society but they are crying in the wilderness as police are winning the propaganda war. Some significant progress, however, has been made with the recent passing of the Coroners Act and the Anti Torture Act. Police will no longer investigate summary executions carried out by their colleagues; an independent coroner will take care of that. Both Acts have potential to compensate victims and address impunity if properly implemented. However, legislation alone will not bring change if it is not accompanied by a societal attitudinal change that states that every suspect is entitled to due process in a court of law.

Kenya must implement the TJRC report
(July 22 2017)

November 3 1994 is a day that may remain etched in my memory for ever perhaps. On that fateful day, a priest colleague of mine, Martin Boyle, left our Nairobi home and set out alone on the journey back to his parish in Nandi. He arrived a week later in a coffin. Martin was pursued by a chasing vehicle, forced off the Nakuru highway and shot dead in broad daylight on Limuru Road. His car was not stolen, nor were its contents interfered with. His killers drove away unimpeded. The entire incident was witnessed by a Good Samaritan who stopped and tried to assist him. No real investigations were done and the church did not pursue the matter with any vigour although everyone agreed that it was a targeted killing. Martin had spent 26 years in Nandi and Elgeyo Marakwet building schools and clinics as well as churches. He was a powerful figure who had infuriated the power [barons] in both places. I thought of him again recently as the country laid to rest a handful of figures mentioned adversely in the Truth, Justice and Reconciliation Commission (TJRC) report. Martin's murder troubles me because we have had no closure on his assassination. Hundreds of Kenyan families have had no closure either with regard to the slaughter of their loved ones in Wagalla, Kiambaa, Nyayo chambers and elsewhere. The Jubilee government promised but failed to deliver on the implementation of the TJRC report. Now Mr Ruto has dismissed calls to implement the report claiming it would create disharmony and divide Kenyans along tribal lines. He wants everyone to "accept and move on". Dismissing the right of victims to access truth, justice and public acknowledgment displays sheer contempt and poor leadership. If you fear truth and justice then you have something to hide or else you are protecting the perpetrators of heinous crimes. You certainly are not on the side of victims. We have become used to this false 'peace' that Mr Ruto advocates. It is a strange type of calm, where we dare not disrupt the State narrative that all is well as we march ahead, hand in hand. The Jews wanted a saviour like that who would be peaceful, subdued and not upset the status quo. Instead, they got a man who bluntly informed them, 'Do not suppose that I have come to bring peace to the earth. I did not come to bring peace to the earth, but a sword' (Mt 10:34). He also said the truth will set you free, but politicians propose and prefer servitude. Northern Ireland too attempted to deal with the past by just looking forward. It created a power sharing government, reformed institutions and peace agreements but never dealt with the past. It got solutions without agreeing what the problem was. But families are demanding truth about the 'disappeared' and resources and devolved government are in tatters. There is no avoidance of an ugly past. The TJRC report was flawed but it is a start and very soon we must look back if we are to truly move forward.

Christmas message can inspire revolution
(December 23 2017)

In the silence of the night, an infant that would inspire, instruct, provoke and challenge the religious and secular authorities of his day and every generation thereafter was born. No fanfare, no media announcement, no Facebook page or Instagram — not even 'chai ya mtoto'. Instead, the son of Mary secretly sneaked unannounced into the messiness of human existence and immersed himself in the lives of the lowly, the forgotten and the rejected. There he found a home and gave meaning and hope to those who never get to share in the wealth and decision-making on this earth. It was not by chance that Jesus was born in destitution, far from home and in a stable because there was no welcome in Bethlehem for a woman about to deliver her first child. Those chosen to be the first to hear of the birth were the despised, distrusted shepherds — the matatu touts of their day. His option for the poor was palpable from day one. As he launched his ministry 30 years later, Jesus announced that he had come to bring good news to the poor, to set captives and the downtrodden free, proclaiming a year of favour. He lived a life of service and simplicity right up to his humiliation and rejection on the cross. His resurrection gave a whole new meaning to his teachings and became the inspiration for the movement that he started. Two thousand years later, we have clothed Jesus in glory and sanitised his message. The bold, compassionate, confrontational Son of Man has been tamed, frequently locked up in tabernacles far away from the mud and stench of the market place where he chose to hang out. Instead of opting for the poor, most churches preach a prosperity gospel. Jesus is the new witch doctor, they proclaim. Give tithe, get saved and get rich. A simple message that somehow does not explain why over half the population is still poor and yet churches are overflowing. But it might explain how some church leaders amass wealth. Politicians, too, have hijacked the Jesus project, attributing their success, mansions, helicopters and votes to their dependency on God. It is fashionable to display your wealth and proclaim your faith. A year of politics has left the nation divided and the poor disenchanted. Christmas reminds us that while Jesus was born for all of us, he has particular mercy and love for the downcast and the downtrodden. Put another way, he came to comfort the afflicted and to afflict the comfortable. That is revolutionary. Jesus knew that change would not come from the top. It is only those who have endured hardship and exclusion that are really ready to embrace change in leadership and vision. The status quo will resist change as the State is captive to cartels at national and county levels. Jesus preached revolution — of minds and hearts. That is the basis for structural and leadership transformation. There are no saviours en route to save this country. We are the ones we have been waiting for and God is on the side of the poor, not the powerful. That is still the message coming from Bethlehem. Peace to people of Goodwill and Merry Christmas.

Black lives should matter in Kenya, too (January 6 2018)

It has become fashionable for footballers to make the sign of the cross as they enter the playing field. In Kenya, however, our most fervent prayers are preserved for those occasions when we enter public transport vehicles or when we are about to hit the road. Every time you undertake a long-distance journey, you put your life in your hands. Kenya's roads have become a battlefield for the war fought by the twin forces of speed and greed, with the latter determining the former. Thousands of Kenyans are slaughtered, maimed and traumatised each year, sacrificed at the altars of quick profit while their government remains indifferent because most politicians, public officials and police officers have shares in the transport industry and are not going to let a few hundred more deaths put their earnings at risk. It is the poor who use public transport, who die in the road carnage and the poor again who pay double when their government bans night travel. The slaughter at Migaa is a reflection of what is wrong with our society. The lives of the poor rarely matter except at election time when their numbers are needed at rallies, ballots and protests. Bloggers and activists have called for heads to roll at the National Transport and Safety Authority (NTSA) but don't expect Mr Uhuru Kenyatta to take corrective action over the latest slaughter. Just recall a few weeks ago that he praised the police for their professional performance during the election period, a time when they killed over a 100 of his citizens. The other day, Nyeri town MP Ngunjiri Wambugu posted on his Twitter account that he believes that not one of those who died in that violence was innocent — not even baby Pendo, I guess. This is the man who came to prominence campaigning for ICC to investigate the killings during the post-election violence of 2008. When American police torture an African-American, Kenyans join the world in insisting that Black Lives Matter. But when Kenyan police gun down suspects, the same Kenyans remain silent as if black lives in Kenya don't matter. Worse still, many applaud when the police kill suspects that later are often found to be unarmed. The right to respect and to life applies to everyone. These rights go to the deserving as well as the undeserving. That is the message of the Gospel and the Constitution. The poor deserve to live life in its fullness not because they have earned it, but because they are human like you and I. But when 45 per cent of the nation remains locked in poverty, who is going to protest when a few thousand more die on our roads or from a rogue police officer's bullet? The poor also die in collapsed buildings and out of neglect when sick. The shameful row over the ownership of the St Mary Hospitals will almost certainly result in the poor not being able to access those quality services any more. Leadership from the top is required urgently to bring discipline, order and equality to public life. Dr Fred Matiang'i has shown that it is possible to reverse the rot. But even his efforts, like those of John Michuki before him, may come to nothing if his boss does not support a radical transformation of every ministry.

SELECTED COLUMNS IN
THE EAST AFRICAN STANDARD
MARCH 2018 – MARCH 2020

Clerical culture breeds impunity in our churches
(May 20 2018)

Kenyans are beaten numb and dumb with endless exposés on financial scandals that have characterised successive regimes since independence. Yet the political class [has] no monopoly on scams and scandals. Churches locally and globally are frequently coming under scrutiny from their faithful and the law and they too are often found wanting when it comes to accountability, cover ups, sexual abuse and misuse of power. Faith institutions have traditionally been places of refuge and sanctuary, beacons of hope amid chaos, darkness and despair; but not anymore, or certainly not to the same extent. People everywhere are asking questions on how institutions that claim to be founded by God and guided by Holy Books could be corrupted just like any other organisation. Many respond by saying that institutions may of course be divine in origin but run by mere mortals and so are prone to sin. Point taken, but the question is, what sort of clerical culture breeds abuse and then attempts to cover up the same crimes thus denying victims both justice and safety? The issue at stake is not so much why evil happens but what the leadership response to such crimes is. Some reckon that there is so much impunity in faith organisations that religious people can literally get away with murder. The most poignant moment in an ordination ceremony is when the candidates prostrate themselves on the ground in an act of obedience, submission and humility. The act is meant to symbolise a commitment to service, simplicity and humility. Yet, its symbolism is often lost amid the other elements that point to an extravagant show of triumphalism that indicates that the candidates are rather special and have made it. This is a far cry from the washing of the feet example of Jesus in John 13. In fact, the pastor or priest emerges from such ceremonies as a different creature altogether. They are given a title, new dress and new privileges. These all symbolise the new club that they have joined. They have not yet merited such privileges but they can be tempted to presume that they are special as the masses address them differently and relate to them accordingly. The privileges they receive can soon be considered deserved rewards or entitlements just like the religious hypocrisy Jesus raged against in Matthew 23. They now have new powers and knowledge not accorded to the faithful and they also have a new found status because they are doing the work of God. They can then become distinct, set apart because they have passed through the door and been admitted by those already on the inside. Of course, their role is different and unique but this tempts many to believe that they are special, superior to the masses and accountable only to God. This is the origins of a culture that is clerical but destructive. Convinced about their special-ness many are sensitive to any criticism and don't see any need to consult or seek approval on decisions since Father or Pastor knows best. When the culture deteriorates secrecy and lack of accountability for funds and behaviour are evident. But what happens when offences are noted and reported? Regretfully often the matter is dealt with internally and covered up so as to not to spoil the good name of the church or to scandalise the faithful. So, the offender is transferred to reoffend elsewhere and the victims are left paying the price and often holding the baby. The followers too of course cooperate and tolerate this culture rather than confronting the leadership. But sooner or later the truth emerges and the whole body of the church is blamed for the crime of a few reckless individuals. If anything can be learned from the experience of others in this regard it is that the longer scandals go unaddressed the greater the danger for vulnerable victims and the greater the cost for churches when the extent of abuse is revealed. Pope Francis has stated his intention to remove from office any Bishop who covers up sexual abuse against children and vulnerable adults. The Anglican Church in Tasmania is selling off half of its churches to compensate victims of child sexual abuse. This can be avoided in Kenya if leadership is willing to act decisively, justly and promptly and respond to the cries of victims. A crime is a crime whether committed by a Bishop, Pastor or a Prophet. None of us is above the law.

Access to quality contraceptives will cut abortions (July 1 2018)

No subject raises such strong feelings and emotions like that of abortion. Bring the topic up at the village bar or local fellowship and rest assured you will not find agreement or harmony among those present. Abortion is an emotive issue because it touches the core, our very definitions and understanding of life as well as the rights of women and the unborn. These rights are rarely balanced to the satisfaction of all parties. To address the subject in a platform such as this is also risky yet we cannot ignore the topic nor regard it as a private matter. No matter how well intentioned we might be, abortion can never be reduced to a matter of choice or preference because it affects another human being. The figures for induced abortions in Kenya are staggering. It is estimated that 464,000 induced abortions are completed each year. That is 48 per 1,000 women in the national population. That research was done in 2012 and other results from the same study revealed that 49 per cent of all pregnancies were unintended while 41 per cent of those unintended pregnancies ended up in abortion. Yet irrespective of one's position those figures are dangerously high especially when we consider that most abortions are done in backstreet clinics with crude instruments that put women's lives in danger. In [a] 2008 documentation, East Africa had the highest global rates of unsafe abortions at 36 per 1,000 women. Done unsafely the subject was one of the most contentious in the drafting of the 2010 Constitution. In the end this is what the approved law had to say in Article 26 (4): Abortion is not permitted unless in the opinion of a trained health professional, there is need for emergency treatment, or the life of the mother is in danger, or if permitted by any other law. In other words, there are three provisions under which abortion can legally take place. In 2012 the Ministry of Health provided some guidelines for legal abortions which are in accordance with the Constitution. Yet, further studies reveal that even today 50 per cent of Kenyan abortions are done unsafely. Yet most will agree that abortions are far too many and that it is in everyone's interest that they be reduced. That is not impossible even in societies where abortion is legal and free. In 2015 the rate of abortions in America dropped to its lowest level since the Roe v Wade ruling that legalised it in 1973. In that year the figure stood at 16.3 per 1.000 women. That later peaked at 29.6 in 1981. However, in 2015 the figure had dropped to 14.6. Put another way, in 1990 there were 1.6 million abortions in America but in 2014 there were 926,000 - a significant drop. Of course, the reasons for the fall are also contested. Some suggest that the main cause was that sentiment had turned against abortion. Others claim that the decline is due to the requirement for all to have an Ultrasound test, a result of which many would thereafter decide not to proceed with the abortion since they have witnessed the development of the foetus. However, there is a third opinion that might explain the reduction and that is the greater access to family planning and contraceptives to the general population in the USA. What cannot be doubted is that there are fewer unintended pregnancies and that can only be a good thing. Put another way, high levels of abortion rates correspond to high levels of unmet contraceptive need. Further research reveals that 58 per cent of Kenyan women use some form of contraception. That figure may be rising but it hardly does justice to women and almost certainly explains why there are so many abortions. Fifty years ago, the Catholic Church failed to take the advice of its own experts and produced a document called Humanae Vitae that rejected all forms of contraception except what was called the 'natural method during the safe period'.

The Magisterium expected loving relationships to be regulated around calendars, thermometers and mucus. It was like approving Russian roulette and has been disastrous for couples all over the globe. Most in their wisdom ignored the teaching. However, much more is required. Firstly, I believe Pope Francis is humble enough to apologise for the horrible error of teaching and judgment. Secondly, Catholic health facilities all over the globe should provide access to contraception to all whom it serves. After all, each unintended pregnancy has a 25 per cent chance of ending up as an abortion. Do we want that?

Without talk on social justice and inequality, the handshake is futile (September 16 2018)

Absent from the frontline for a few moons, I have upon return made a point of asking Kenyans what they now make of the famous March 9 handshake between Raila Odinga and Uhuru Kenyatta. Interestingly, almost everyone approves of the gesture of friendship even if no one can explain what the handshake was about nor the benefit it has brought six months after its surprise occurrence. Most welcome the March ceasefire with relief rather than excitement since political and ethnic tension has reduced and Kenyans can resume normal relations and [friendships] with their neighbours. Kenyans no longer feel the need to defend their ethnic identity or apologise for the failings of their leaders. They are much more likely to admit that ethnic political barons have been playing games with their votes and minds for far too long. They point to the fact that as in 2008, the elites [ended] up drinking tea together and sharing the spoils while Wanjiku and Atieno [ended] up poor or in prison for their misguided support of their ethnic leaders. That is one major outcome of the March 9 encounter. While most then breathe a sigh of relief few, want to discuss the credibility of last year's ballot, nor the IEBC nor even justice for Chris Msando's family. That is the amnesia dimension to the handshake. Even Opposition parties have gone silent on these issues. The Building Bridges Team have made little impact either and resembles the National Cohesion and Integration Commission (NCIC) agency lacking any justice agenda. Who talks about justice these days? The silence of the Opposition confirms that they are just cut from the same cloth as Jubilee. The only difference is the ethnic and geographical factor. In terms of ideology, values and lifestyle they are all the same. ODM is still waiting and wondering what 'Baba' has to say before speaking on any issue of national importance, including the 16 per cent VAT on fuel. Of course, there will always be a minority of MPs from all the parties who retain a national agenda and who are mindful of the poor and dispossessed of the nation. But unless they combine their forces, they will not impact greatly. What the handshake has demonstrated is that ethnicity is not the number one problem in the country. Inequality is, and the elected representatives are for the most part unwilling to address the glaring inequality that divides and impoverishes the nation in a way that ethnicity never does. Inequality is left unaddressed because it exposes the great class divide that is maintained and safeguarded by the ruling political and property-owning class of the nation. To speak of social justice is to challenge the status quo and politicians are not ready to surrender their privileges and perks to share the national cake with the underprivileged. Religious leaders convened a National Dialogue Conference at Ufungamano House this week. Their initiative attempted to compliment the Building Bridges plan while reminding the handshake team that nothing credible or commendable has emerged in six months from that team. However, neither team appears willing to tackle the issues of inequality and social justice. There was no outrage on the podium about the cost of sugar, flour or cooking oil. The national debt is at Sh5 trillion and the burden of repayment is passed not onto those who incurred the loans or looted their share but to those who are least able to pay – the poor and unemployed. It is likely that the amount looted from national coffers and laundered in real estate at home and abroad is greater than the national debt. Will religious leaders speak about that? Tribalism is just a facade to conceal looting and the enslavement of the poor, who are found in equal measure in every ethnic group. Only the emergence of a strong social movement that gives them space and a voice can seriously challenge the status quo and bring about change. Harriett Tubman said, 'I freed a thousand slaves, I could have freed thousands more if only they knew they were slaves'. This is the national dialogue that is required.

Giving is not a problem, Ruto, the razzmatazz over your generosity is (November 11 2018)

For a quarter of a century the national broadcaster, KBC, religiously informed us on the Sunday evening news where President Moi attended church that particular day. That church service took precedence over every local or global event no matter how important that was. The absence of Mr Moi on any given Sunday often caused enormous speculation. Things have changed but not radically. Every Sunday, bulletins still carry up to a half dozen items on what the political class preached when they attended church that day. They will be seen addressing the faithful from the pulpit, sanctuary or at the church entrance. But the first message to be conveyed is that our politicians are God fearing people. In recent times, another item of curiosity for many is with regard to the amount that Deputy President William Ruto donated to a particular church. Some keep records of his generosity and speculate as to the source of that enormous wealth. However, Mr Ruto is not deterred by the criticism and insists that he will continue to support churches since he is giving back to God and investing in the hereafter. Generosity is indeed the hallmark of the Christian. Paul instructs the Corinthians (2 Corinthians 9:7) that the Lord loves a cheerful giver. However, it is not what you do but the way that you do it that pleases God if we are to heed the wisdom of the New Testament. For Christians, their Constitution is the Sermon on the Mount. Jesus had a lot to say about giving when he ascended the mountain without the assistance of a microphone or a recording by TV cameras. In Chapter 6:1-4 of Matthew's Gospel, Jesus insists that our good deeds should not be done so that people can see them. If that is our intent, then we have already received our reward, the applause and the approval of the people. When we give alms, we should not blow a trumpet about it as the hypocrites do to win the praise of others. Instead, we should not let our left hand know what our right hand is doing 'so that your alms giving must be secret and your Father who sees in secret will repay you'. The message here is stop the fanfare, the razzmatazz, the circus. If Mr Ruto or any other public figure wants to give, then let it be done secretly and privately away from the cameras and the praise singers. When you give publicly, you are only blowing your own trumpet and getting recognition. In the process, you are buying popularity and indebting the recipients to you. Put another way, giving like this is a power thing and the beneficiaries are being compromised in one way or another; through silence, acquiescence, support or prayers. For Jesus the issue is not giving then, but the intent. Why are you giving and why so publicly? The beautiful story of the Widow's mite in Mark 12: 41-44 illustrates the importance of sincerity where the rich are reminded that despite the large amounts they have donated, the widow gave more than any of them since they gave from their surplus, but she contributed all that she had. That gives perspective to the millions dished out each weekend. Jesus continuously raged against hypocrisy. In Matthew 23, he attacks the religious leaders of the day by claiming, 'all their works are performed to be seen... they love places of honour at banquets, seats of honour in synagogues, greetings in marketplaces and the salutation 'Rabbi'. This makes one wonder why politicians get front seats in churches and can't pray without being recorded by the cameras. Yet church people who permit politicians to desecrate the sanctuary are equally responsible for allowing churches to sanitise the wealth of figures with whom the public have serious issues of integrity. If one third of the annual budget goes unaccounted for each year, then those who hold the highest echelons of power must be the first suspects in the looting spree. When these same individuals now parade their good deeds in our churches, the pastor becomes an accomplice in the cover up and the [church] an obstacle towards alleviating the evil that is corruption. For these reasons any church that is committed to the teachings of Jesus should not invite nor permit politicians to bail them out of poverty or to take over their sacred spaces in church.

Stop burning bridges and building new ones, implement TJRC report (November 18 2018)

The Building Bridges Initiative (BBI) team were due in the Coast last week. However, at the last minute, the Malindi and Mombasa meetings were cancelled due to lack of resources. This surprised some but amused others. Eight months after its formation, the team that emerged from the March 9 handshake cannot afford to travel to the Coast despite the importance of the mandate that we are frequently reminded about. Even Wanjiku can afford the SGR and BBI could have experienced at first-hand Chinese efficiency and punctuality. Coast hospitality would have been happy to help out with 'chai na mahamri' while tents and chairs could be hired for the price of a single air ticket. Choreographed plot All jokes aside, the only ones bothered about the postponement were the region's politicians. One governor was quoted as saying he and his followers had prepared extensive memoranda for the meeting in Malindi and another was cited as saying that a referendum is inevitable. When politicians get excited about a particular project, they know something you don't. That being the case, you need to be cautious and suspicious. The BBI might well prove a carefully choreographed plot with an outcome that is predetermined. You may well be invited along to rubber stamp a project that betrays your interests and those of the public good. Suspicion abounds mainly because Kenyans still don't know what the handshake was all about. It did lead to a reduction in political tension, but beyond a few jobs for the protagonists and annihilating the Opposition in the process, the details of the deal remain secretive, unclear or are still a work in progress. Yet the demand to change the constitution has gained momentum and it appears we are being bullied and hurried into a referendum the public has not requested. That is not to suggest that the constitution is perfect. But to ask honestly and fairly, what problems bedevil the nation that only constitutional amendments can address? Think about that for a while and reflect on the challenges of corruption, insecurity, inequality, poverty, national debt, wastage, cost of living, food shortages, climate change and unemployment. Will an amendment be a silver bullet for any of those problems? Put another way, all of those issues could be addressed tomorrow by the institutions and resources currently available if there [was] political will. We don't need to reinvent the wheel, but to get the wheels of government and justice moving in the right direction at top speed. In other words, preparing another series of memoranda for the BBI team is an absolute waste of time and energy. We have spent decades creating commissions of inquiry, spending long hours giving views and proposals, creating volumes of reports that are not implemented. We should not be fooled again. President Uhuru Kenyatta and Raila Odinga should first tell us when they will establish a team to implement the Truth, Justice and Reconciliation Commission (TJRC) report. Perhaps then the public may take them seriously. How can you decide to sidestep the crimes of the past and talk of building bridges towards a better tomorrow? The impression we get is that the Raila–Kenyatta team are burning bridges behind them and then constructing new ones to unknown destinations. The hardest thing to learn in life is to know which bridges to cross and which bridges to burn behind us. The BBI team would be well advised to consider this wisdom. Kenyans are being forced to move ahead and accept that handshakes buried the past crimes. In any case, if they require further resources or reports they could shake the dust [off] volumes of the Ndung'u Commission of Inquiry into land grabbing or the Waki Report on Election Violence or even the Akiwumi Commission Report on Ethnic Land Clashes. Resolving the nation's problems is not rocket science, nor does it require a team of eminent retired elders earning fat, sitting allowances at taxpayers' expense. It needs serious people committed to change and addressing the nation's ills. Don't be fooled by this team, demand implementation of the constitution and commission.

Time for Mazrui Trust to do justice to rightful land owners in Coast (December 16 2018)

How often have you heard administrators, politicians and even presidents tell you that they are going to solve the land problem in Kenya? Does anyone believe them anymore? We have half a dozen commission reports on the land question gathering dust, only accessed by foreigners or academics writing their theses. We are not short of documentation or recommendations. What we are missing is honesty, sincerity and commitment from the political class and aggressive activism from the dispossessed victims. Politicians exhaustively talk about fighting corruption, but how many of them acknowledge that the rot in public life and the looting of the coffers have their genesis in the theft of public land. Generations of politicians since independence have gotten rich by grabbing land, and Mr Kenyatta knows that only too well. The thieves only turned to stealing from parastatals and ministries when the land bank dried up. The land question at the coast is well-documented, but the politicians only bring it up at election time. However, it was surprisingly interesting to hear Kilifi Governor Amason Kingi for the first time since he assumed office in 2013, speak passionately, boldly and constructively about the troubles that have be-devilled his constituents for centuries. His paper, submitted to the Building Bridges Initiative team, was also shared through national newspapers. Only time will tell whether Mr Kingi will maintain his energy on the subject after the handshake team moves to the next destination. For half a century, Kilifi politicians have complained about the landlessness and squatter problem, but most betrayed their people and were bought to silence with plum jobs or 10 acres of land. The history of the indigenous people in the county for the past centuries is one of appalling subjugation, deprivation and enslavement. With the arrival of the Arabs, they were forced to move to the hinterland to escape slavery. With the abolition of slavery, they attempted to repossess their land, but thanks to the connivance of the British and the Sultan of Zanzibar, the 10-mile strip was handed over to the Mazrui Trust. The 1888 and 1895 agreements terminated the land rights of the indigenous and half-hearted and mischievous opportunities for them to re-stake claim on the land by virtue of the Land Titles Ordinance of 1908 were thwarted by the Mazrui family who secured 77,000 acres for themselves in Central Kilifi, as well as gaining 95 per cent of Malindi. The British fully supported this land grab because they wanted to prop up the aristocratic ex slave owners and develop plantations. In the process, the indigenous were regarded as only suitable as labourers for the plantation owners. The Mijikenda then went from slaves to squatters or 'watumwa wa siri' (secret slaves) and even today, they still don't possess titles or security of tenure. Adjudication in 1989: Parliament enacted the Mazrui Trust Repeal Act, which purported to pave the way for the adjudication of the land. However, in 2012, that was reversed on the grounds that the land was not Trust Land, but was now under the Waki Commission. The struggle for justice however continues and my colleagues at Haki Yetu, working together with the local land committee, petitioned Parliament this year over the matter. They then invited the Parliamentary Lands Committee to visit the ground and listen to representatives of 10,000 families in Takaungu. Recently, the same committee invited the Mazrui Trust to Parliament. We await the report of the Parliamentary Committee whose members include Owen Baya, the Kilifi North MP who has displayed enthusiasm for the cause. The Mazrui family have [been] ordered to surrender some of the land with the proviso that the National Land Commission (NLC) should compensate them. They made no reference to the right of the indigenous to receive compensation for the centuries of enslavement and the expropriation of their ancestral land. One should expect that the commission would address the community's grievances. On the contrary, however, NLC chairman Mohamed Swazuri, wrote a letter of approval to the Mazrui Trust to illegally hive off 2,380 acres as leasehold to Mombasa Cement company, a decision that has led petitioners to write to Parliament to have him removed from the commission on grounds of graft. Kingi wants the NLC to be completely disbanded. Meanwhile, the Mazrui Trust must not be permitted to retain vast tracts of land to dispose of as they wish while the owners live in abject poverty in a new form of slavery as squatters.

Finally, Vatican acts on sexual abuse, but is it really enough? (February 24 2019)

Theodore McCarrick will go down in history as the first Cardinal to be dismissed from the clerical state in the Catholic Church. The once mighty prelate has dramatically fallen from grace; his defrocking handed down by Pope Francis for the cardinal sins of abuse of children and vulnerable adults in America. The Pontiff may have dallied in addressing these horrific crimes, but with the dismissal of McCarrick, he is now stating categorically that not even princes of the church are above the law. That every cleric is called to integrity, accountability and protection of children and vulnerable adults. Yet, Francis is only too aware that defilement of children and adults is causing as much pain, shame and disgrace in the Catholic

Church as the anguish of division caused by the Reformation 500 years ago. What initially appeared like 'a few bad apples' in the English-speaking countries, has surfaced in every corner of the [globe as a church problem] that can no longer be swept under the carpet. For decades, paedophilia was not understood as the sickness that it is and few grasped how predators destroy their young victims' lives. Offenders were transferred to other stations where most continued their abuse on vulnerable children. Bishops covered up to protect the good name of the Church which took precedence over justice for the victims. But with each passing week, more revelations and scandals hit the headlines and the church no longer has a good name in much of the world. The Pope has now called the leaders of the church to Rome for a four-day meeting to reflect on the crisis. Expectations are high that the church will put in place policies to protect children, remedies to address the past and punishment for those who have abused. Victims will be granted opportunities to share their stories and press upon leaders that cover-ups, indifference and silence will no longer be tolerated. It is hoped all those who attend will return home and start a process of discussion, redress and justice for victims in every diocese in the world. The silence must give way to open and frank investigations and discussions at every level to ensure every child and adult is safe in the Catholic Church. Of course, there are many who will be uncomfortable with hearing about the sins in the church. There are those who might even believe that my writing on the subject is letting the side down, is rocking the boat and displaying our dirty linen in public for people of other denominations and faiths to insult or attack the Catholic Church. However, if the alternative is silence, covering up and secret payments, we all better speak. Our first and primary obligation is to safeguard children and the more that we discuss that in every forum, the safer our young ones will be. Jesus said that the truth will set us free (John 8:32) no matter how painful that is. Incremental change is not enough and piecemeal reforms mere band aid solutions to festering problems that can destroy the church everywhere, and here too. There must be 'zero tolerance' for sexual abuse if the church is to regain credibility and be faithful to its founder. The culture of clericalism, where ordained ministers have been given special powers and protection is at the heart of the rot. Clericalism circles the wagons for those on the inside, but denies justice and protection to those outside. All remedies then cannot be entrusted to clerics alone to oversee and implement. Professional, committed laity everywhere must not only play the watchdog role, but guide policy, supervise clergy and investigate, with the police, complaints that are forwarded. We must [see the] traditional monarchical model of church being replaced by a more democratic, inclusive and accountable one. Pope Francis is a global leader, arguably the only one who speaks with authority on issues of migrants, the environment and the poor while speaking for persecuted Christians in the Middle East and confronting demagogues in the political sphere. The crisis of abuse that he inherited from his predecessors is still a work in progress. He needs prayers and support. For all of us, the big question remains, how safe are our children in churches, schools, sports grounds and our homes? Abuse unfortunately is found everywhere.

Has Uhuru forgotten his promise to victims of State violence? (March 31 2019)

It may have slipped your notice but Sunday last, March 24 was International Right to Truth Day. The day was marked in a low-key manner in Kenya but that does not signify that victims of torture, human rights violations, massacres and detention have lost hope and chosen the 'accept and move on' mantra that Jubilee scripted. Impoverished by suffering emanating from state violations, few survivors can afford to travel to the capital to express their desperation and pain. But that should not be taken to mean that they have forgotten or forgiven. March 24 was chosen as Right to Truth Day because in 1980 Archbishop Oscar Romero was gunned down in his Cathedral in San Salvador as he said mass while preaching against state atrocities. Romero was canonised a Saint by Pope Francis on October 14 last year, but the man of God would have been embarrassed by such an honour as his reward and joy was only to serve and speak truth to power. Those in power today who believe that peace can be created by a mere handshake would well be advised to listen to the words of Romero from the grave who said, 'Peace is not the product of terror. Peace is not the silence of cemeteries. Peace is not the silent result of violent repression. Peace is dynamism. Peace is generosity. It is [a] right and it is a duty'. The peace that we are consistently reminded exists then is a mere tranquiliser that induces us to forget about the past and allow perpetrators go scot free. Yes, the Kenyan government has had difficulty in dealing with the past and the truth for half a century. Survivors and families of victims are tired of hearing politicians talking about the danger of opening up old wounds. But those wounds will not heal by themselves. They need treatment without which the infection will poison the whole body and the next generation. The Truth Justice and Reconciliation Commission (TJRC) handed over their four-volume report to President Kenyatta on May 21 2013. The TJRC stated that the report should be tabled in Parliament in 21 days and that implementation [should begin] within six months.

Six years later, Mr Kenyatta has chosen to let the report gather dust and appears to not have the slightest intention of establishing a team for its implementation. Proof [that] the Government [fears] its contents and dissemination is shown by the fact that you cannot access the full TJRC report on any government website. You will only acquire it on the website of University of Seattle in Canada where an ex-Commissioner Ron Slye works (https://digitalcommons.law.seattleu.edu/tjrc-core/). More disturbing still is that in the presidential address to the nation in 2015 Kenyatta promised Sh10 billion for a Justice Restoration Fund. Billions have been sunk in non-existent dams but not a penny has been found to give succour, recognition and reparations to the victims of Wagalla, Kiambaa or Nyayo Chambers. Since it assumed power, Jubilee [has] been skirting around the ugly horror stories from the past. The TJRC report was shelved and now we have the Building Bridges Initiative (BBI) which is the new panacea for the nation's ills. The BBI team have just requested a five months extension to 'complete the task.' Yet, there has been little public interest or energy around this handshake project. No interim progress report has been availed and no response made to the growing cynicism about its predetermined outcome that will secure a referendum to create more positions in power for the political elite. Referendums will not address the past nor give justice to its many victims. Failure to implement the TJRC report only advances the culture of impunity at every level. Is it any wonder then that looting has reached an all-time high and that extra judicial killings are as frequent as they have ever been? The poor are almost always the victims and illegal evictions continue unabated. It is shocking to think that half a century after independence that the government treats its own citizens as [badly] as the colonial administration. KHRC went to London to get compensation and justice for the Mau Mau torture victims. Where will Kenyans go to demand what they are entitled to? Not dealing with the past is a sure guarantee of the same crimes repeated in this generation. There are no short cuts in this respect. Romero said those of us who have a voice must continue to speak for these voiceless victims.

Jubilee regime must awaken to reality of waning public trust
(May 5 2019)

Despite the lack of clear, consistent information on Huduma Namba registration, people continue to spend hours waiting in line to participate in the process. Kenyans are a compliant people - some might say docile - when it comes to following government announcements. Perhaps it is the fear of exclusion – a remnant of colonialism – that guides participation in the process rather than enthusiasm for a national project that few have any genuine confidence in. A mother told me recently that it took 14 months to get a birth certificate for her son, reason being that there was no printing paper at the local Huduma Centre. So, it is not surprising that she has little confidence that the Huduma Namba project will improve services for her family. Whatever your opinion, you must acknowledge that there is a shortage of trust and a lot of suspicion around this exercise. The basic question is why Huduma Namba is needed at all. The government already has the same information and many countries, including my own, have survived very nicely without any national identity card. Raila Odinga agreed to put his face on billboards to encourage his supporters to get registered. The NASA team were dispatched to strategic locations on the opening day along with a bevy of media houses to garner support. But William Ruto's absence in Kakamega and his reticent backing for the exercise spoke volumes. His guarded approval resonates with many people. Constantly, I hear questions as to whether this is a pre-census exercise that will ensure that those communities that appeared to double and triple between the 1999 and 2009 censes will be finally cut down to size. Others believe that the outcome could be used to manipulate figures and boundaries in the other very expensive project slated for this year, that of reviewing constituency boundaries to be implemented by the IEBC. In the event of a referendum also taking place and the outcome being a decision to go for a parliamentary system with an executive prime minister, then issues of numbers and distribution of constituencies could become a very contested and controversial issue. This is not being alarmist but the talk on the ground. Indeed, there is just as much suspicion and dissatisfaction around the Building Bridges Initiative (BBI). With its opaqueness and extension until the year end, many are sceptical about the independence of the BBI team, believing that they are just waiting for the nod at the appropriate time from their masters to announce that a referendum is scheduled. Yet the question and perhaps the outcome are already predetermined. This may appear to be a cynical and negative analysis of what is going on. However, what is apparent is that the public have less and less trust in this regime's leadership. There is a huge deficit of trust and that should be a concern for the Jubilee administration. A further illustration of this is the resistance to the payment of the proposed housing levy. Taxpayers are far from convinced that this is a valuable, necessary or honest project. To give more of your hard-earned cash to the treasury with the remote hope that you will acquire a home on a lottery basis is not just madness; it is no better than the online sports gambling that has tricked the nation. No wonder then that people have doubts whether they can trust the government with their taxes or with their personal information. The public are more and more aware of the flaws, divisions, fraud and theft that have characterised successive administrations. They may not be rushing to the streets to protest but they are bitterly angry that the compulsory deductions from their meagre salaries is being looted on a mega scale and that a pittance comes back in services and in church collections to buy the acquiescence of the religious class. Jubilee must awaken to the knowledge that trust in their leadership is fast disappearing. The silence of the church and the once formidable political opposition should not be read as indifference or approval. Resistance may not come the Sudan or Algerian way but it nevertheless exists. The rising cost of food items was the beginning of the Sudan revolt and the message here is to be very, very cautious. All the public are waiting for is an alternative leadership that may offer greater accountability, leadership and justice and they will move in that direction. The chances of that happening may not be as remote as some people think.

We may feel obliged to do census but who really counts in Kenya?
(September 1 2019)

Yesterday was the last opportunity to be included in this year's census. Not sure if that matters to most citizens because the majority took part out of a sense of duty, maybe even fear, rather than conviction that this is an important exercise that adds value to their lives or one that will improve service delivery. Yet, censuses have been on record ever since Joseph and Mary had to leave Galilee and join the headcount in Bethlehem (Luke 2:1). Then each had to return to their home district for the count, so at least Kenyans were spared that inconvenience and expense last weekend. But globally, censuses have been shown to be as much about politics, race and ethnicity as about national planning and values. America for decades had been recording the [skin colour] of its citizens and when that was deemed politically incorrect Donald Trump attempted unsuccessfully to have a question inserted in next year's census about nationality. South Africa in the Apartheid years used the regular census as a means to pigeon-hole its citizens into race and colour boxes. Statistics and data revealed should always be used positively but more often than not have been used as a means of control and manipulation of certain sections of society. As Kenya comes to grips with the toxic ethnic factor in politics, inheritance, wealth and job distribution, does it make moral sense to ask its citizens to reveal their ethnic identity. Why would that question be of importance in an exercise that claims to be about enhancing national identity? Who could possibly justify or benefit from compiling figures and percentages of the nation's forty something ethnic communities? Questions on access to computer services or online shopping are mere insults to the nation's 40 per cent living in poverty not to mention the 2.5 million reported this week at risk of starvation. This year's census will cost the nation $180 million or Sh18 billion. Surely that amount could have been put to better use to feed the hungry or educate the poor. Yet, we are supposed to applaud when told that we have participated in another first as a paperless census. The country spent another Sh8 billion just a few months ago on a fairly similar futile exercise called biometric registration. The new generation Huduma Cards were to be distributed by July but two months later there is not a sign of them on the horizon. The combined cost of the census and biometric registration is $260 million or the equivalent of another wasted Eurobond. To add to the waste and pointlessness we are due to surrender another Sh8 billion to the disgraced and corrupted IEBC to conduct a constituency boundaries review. God help us! We may well discover in a year's time that all three exercises were flawed, manipulated, overpriced and just added to the ethnic political conflicts that have be-devilled the country for half a century. There is no need to spend billions to discover that the population has reached 52 billion and that the number of poor Kenyans continues to grow even if the percentage in destitution has dropped. Recently retired Auditor General Edward Ooko has all the information required to prove that up to 40 per cent of the annual budget is looted. He could also provide information free of charge to the DPP on whom to investigate and take to Kamiti. Yes, before I forget there is the Building Bridges Initiative (BBI) that plans to spend more billions on a referendum that no one has requested. The dynasties and elites want to castrate the Constitution before its 20th birthday. The Turkana oil is shipped to Malaysia of all places to be refined yet a fraction of the money spent on these dubious projects would have built an oil refinery on home soil. Kenya may feel obliged to do an annual census in line with international standards. You may be counted but the larger question is do you count at all? Put another way, who counts and who doesn't in this country? We might be better deployed spending a few million to discuss with the marginalised and the leftovers whether they count or not and if they have a genuine sense of belonging or ownership in this potentially great nation. Their answers might produce more guidance and wisdom than any census might ever contribute. But would that interest the powerful who only need the services of the powerless to wash their clothes, guard their homes and show up on election day?

How the handshake has conspired to kill [the] Mombasa economy (November 3 2019)

The five ferries that traverse the Likoni Channel are a death trap and you take your life in your hands every time you step or drive on board one of them. Three of the ferries do not meet any international safety standards according to a report by Senator Mutula Kilonzo Jr, tabled in Parliament this past week. In the past three years, a whopping Sh600 million has been pumped into the rusting death machines yet it might as well have been dropped in the Indian Ocean for all the difference in safety it has made. The ferries of course are symptomatic of the rot that characterises the state of the once renowned Coastal city. The tourism industry is in ruins with peak season reduced to a few weeks in December when Nairobi moves to Mombasa. Kibarani dumpsite got a face lift that is appreciated by visitors but the tons of garbage have now been transported to residential areas with VOK, Bombolulu a major health hazard to thousands of nearby residents. Transport Cabinet Secretary James Macharia's reluctance to rescind his edict that all imported containers be transported on the SGR has left thousands jobless and led to the relocation of many large businesses to Nairobi and Naivasha. The side effects of course of this action have left many smaller enterprises from food sellers to askaris also losing their only source of income. This is all happening in a period when the country hails a constitution that promised to devolve services and opportunities to enhance development and address economic impoverishment at the local level. Yet, what we are witnessing is quite the opposite. The SGR project has centralised exports and imports in Nairobi and reduced Mombasa to a ghost town. Nobody was consulted nor were alternatives listened to as the government treated with contempt the constitutional mandate to arrange public participation. What is most worrying and revealing is that those who are set to lose the most over the illegal SGR directive are the drivers, brokers, clerks at CFS and those who can't afford to pay rent or school fees. The well-heeled always find other means through their political connections and move [on] to Naivasha, Nairobi or Athi River where they acquire land and resume business. Apart from Mvita MP Abdulswamad Nassir, no politician has come to the defence of the million plus residents [afflicted]. Besides, after one of the recent protest marches, demonstrators marched to the Mombasa governor's office and denounced him for his indifference to their plight. They too are aware that the governor's family transporting business, has reportedly been granted favourable terms to transport their goods on the SGR. Granted, they are not the only company to benefit from this lucrative deal. However, when the elected representative of the city's million plus takes care of [his] family interests before those of his constituents then [who] do you turn to? What the whole scenario does reveal is that there is no opposition to Jubilee left in the country. The only challenge to the ruling party is from within its own walls. The handshake may have removed the threat of street violence but is silent when other protestors are deprived by the police to publicly demonstrate their displeasure over the SGR illegal order. Meetings with Raila Odinga have provided nothing but promises to date for those most affected. With the imminent release of the BBI report it is unlikely that the plight of the suffering in Mombasa will be given any serious attention for the foreseeable future. Makes you wonder whose interests the handshake or the BBI really serves. It is disgraceful however that the poor are made to pay for the mistakes of the powerful. When challenged the powers that be cite the Dongo Kundu by pass and the expected Industrial zone that they claim will provide thousands of jobs when completed. As of now this appears like a pipe dream and cannot in any case repair the damage done by the SGR to the economy, nor address the neglect that is evident all over the second city. Amid the depressing news one must, however, admire the courage and tenacity of the Mombasa protestors who have shown a gritty determination in their struggle. Besides, they are not likely to give up and sooner or later they must get the justice they deserve.

BBI team cannot close eyes to unansweredquestions on land (December 15 2019)

After a quick perusal of the BBI Report upon its initial release, this week I found some precious time to absorb a little more of its contents. Each of us most likely approach such documents with our own personal interests and expectations, and mine centred on what it had to recommend on the issue of land. Half hoping that there might be a chapter devoted to this most sensitive and divisive of matters, the contents page disappointed. Still, when Chapter 1 was entitled, 'Notable issues that Kenyans must deal with' there was hope that gold might be found therein. Alas, after naming 15 issues and not finding land among them, bewilderment set in. Still, better wade through to the end and hope to find some solace and inspiration. No mention of land in Chapter 7 'Shared Prosperity' and wait for it, not a word even in Chapter 8 on 'Corruption'. How in God's name can you produce a 156-page report entitled 'From a Nation of Blood Ties to a Nation of Ideals' and have nothing to say on the matter of land? What about the politically instigated land clashes? What about the land grabbing that was *modus operandi* of the governing elites and their cronies for half a century? This could hardly have been an oversight; more like a deliberate decision to ignore the subject matter! Worse still, sceptics even suspect that the content on land was expunged as it was in the TJRC report. Is the BBI team suggesting that the land question has been resolved and everything is hunky dory? Is there no recognition that there are many unresolved ethnic issues over land ownership? How can they devote a whole chapter on corruption and just dwell on the pilfering of the coffers when the looters only headed there after they had grabbed most of the public land? How can they really talk about addressing inequality and not acknowledge that a few powerful families own up to two million acres of land while the poor are forced to build homes on river banks and slopes prone to landslides? Put another way, does the BBI team believe that land is not a matter that must be dealt with at this time, or do they imagine that it will resolve itself? The only obvious justification for such a grave and deliberate omission must be that the authors did not want to ruffle the feathers of their appointing godfathers. They wanted to present a very sanitised and safe report. In other words, this report was intended for the most part to maintain the status quo and keep wananchi occupied while nothing of substance would really change. When the political class praised the proposed reforms, you can be assured that they see the BBI as a means to consolidate and reinforce their power, not surrender it. When the rest speak of real change, the elites get worried and conspire to silence you. Just in case you suffer from amnesia, the Ndung'u Report revealed that there are 200,000 illegally acquired land titles, whose acreage totals over a million in the hands of thieves. How many of those has the National Land Commission or the EACC repossessed? Advocates of real change should be very angry because the BBI was designed to maintain, not challenge or restrain, the ruling class. This was further evidenced by the decision of two senators and one MP to represent Mike Sonko in court and renege on their sworn constitutional promise to protect the public interest and play their oversight role. That they would attempt to justify their decision just added insult to injury. Perhaps it should not come as a surprise then that the BBI team chose to avoid the sensitive issue of land since members of the ruling class are the principal beneficiaries of the land grabbing culture. But avoidance will not bring resolution and they cannot close their eyes to these unanswered questions: Why are 56 per cent of Nairobi residents still living in slums, 56 years after independence? How can absentee landlords collect rent on land in the Coast and the NLC stands idly by? Why have no efforts been made to implement the Community Land Act, as well-connected individuals still hive [off] huge tracts for themselves? What are recommendations for sharing benefits of county natural resources? Most conflicts in this country have had their roots in the land question. Land and resources are a sitting time bomb that can explode anytime. What is that about Nero fiddling as Rome burned?

Let Coast leaders be sincere on land reform in push to change law (February 2 2020)

The BBI extravaganza was in Mombasa last weekend. It brought much needed revenue to the city with tourism on its deathbed and transport sector crippled thanks to the executive edict that granted SGR a monopoly on transporting goods. The media expected a showdown between the Jubilee factions but they were disappointed. By Monday it was business as usual with the William Ruto group announcing a programme of public meetings to promote its own agenda for reforming the country. Be grateful for the conflict among the political elites, however, because if they were to find agreement on a rushed reform programme this country is doomed. When they discover consensus and shake hands it is almost always to their benefit and to the public's detriment. At least now folk have breathing space to read the task force report if it ever gets published while civil society and the masses have an opportunity to ensure the powerful elites do not mutilate the 2010 Constitution like their forefathers. In the Coast, however, politicians took the opportunity to promote a local agenda for change. Item number one among its 16 points for reform was not surprisingly the issue of land. What was most astounding, however, was that there was not a single mention of land in the 156-page report from the BBI task force. This was clearly a calculated and deliberate omission not an oversight by the task force because the Coastal leaders had submitted the same memorandum in private to the handshake team. Rather than repeat the same agenda in Mama Ngina the Coastal leaders might have been expected to ask publicly why their views on land had been censored in the report. The memorandum had demanded that 'the government must comprehensively address matters of land ownership, titling, management, acquisition and productivity.' They also insisted on the revocation of grants of land to absentee landlords, the suspension of all eviction orders and that expired leases should not be renewed without county government approvals. The issue of historical land injustices in the Coast is an old song every politician sings but no one wants to dance attendance to. The BBI must be the umpteenth forum the same agenda gets the coastal blood boiling for twenty-four hours and thereafter is conveniently removed to the back burner. The elected representatives of the six coastal counties have betrayed their people for decades and failed to push for the implementation of the Njonjo and Ndungu Commissions of Inquiry as well as the TJRC Report. The latter stated unequivocally that 'the communities at the Coast especially the Mijikenda, Taita and Pokomo have suffered the most severe land injustices.' In March 2015 in his state of the nation address, Uhuru Kenyatta established a restorative justice fund of Sh10 billion for the implementation of the TJRC report. Has any coastal MP inquired in Parliament or the Senate as to the whereabouts of that fund? Many expected that when a local person got the chance to head the National Land Commission, he would lead them to the Promised Land but instead he ended up being led to the court cells. A task force was established in 2014 to investigate historical land injustices but instead of producing a Bill for the implementation of their final proposals the report was reduced to a mere Clause as an amendment to the land laws. Clause 44 in the Land Act is vague lacking any institutional or implementation framework. There will always be resistance to addressing the land injustices because the powerful elites have already secured their large tracts of land. But the people's representatives have failed to strategize or to push a common agenda for redress. Was the Mombasa memorandum just more pious aspirations or are [there] politicians more serious this time around? Perhaps if they were sincere about land reform then they would have insisted that the issue of land be withdrawn from the national government and devolved to the counties. Now that would have been a much more controversial amendment to the Constitution than the creation of a third tier of governance to facilitate outgoing governors. It would also have put them at loggerheads with the President and his Deputy who are both accused of denying locals access to water in their huge disputed holdings in Taita Taveta. Are they bold enough?

HOW CAN YOU FORGIVE WHEN YOUR TORMENTOR DOES NOT CONFESS?

The passing of retired President Daniel arap Moi temporarily halted the discussion on BBI but opened up another raging debate on how Kenya has dealt with its past and what the next generation can expect to be taught in history class. While the media heaped praise on Mr Moi those detained under his regime also had their say before he was laid to rest. Many former detainees chose to remain silent, however, and were not photographed in attendance at either of the two funeral ceremonies. Their absence spoke volumes. But for those who chose to comment the public attention was on whether they would forgive Mr Moi.

Forgiveness, as all of us knows, is neither cheap nor easy and goes beyond mere words. It also takes time. As Jesus reminds us, we must forgive seventy times seven (Matthew 18:22). My understanding of this text is that Jesus was advising that we may think that we have forgiven but there are still residues of anger and resentment that come to the surface from time to time and so we have to repeatedly forgive our perpetrator. We may eventually forgive but not forget.

Forgiveness too cannot be forced or staged. Nor can we forgive on behalf of someone else. It is pretty much up to the one who has suffered to make that decision although one's inability or reluctance to forgive can lead to re-traumatisation. So, there is an element of self-interest and preservation when we forgive another. We loosen the shackles that our perpetrator still has over us. At its most basic level forgiveness is the decision not to retaliate or seek revenge for the wrong incurred. That is the theory of course but the reality is quite different for many victims and survivors.

Too often we say let bygones be bygones or forgive and forget. Those cheap clichés fail to appreciate how some have suffered. Of course, if the perpetrators were to seek forgiveness then the victim may respond more favourably. The Catholic tradition of confession and forgiveness addresses this need for some if there is an element of penance and reparation involved. However, when we talk about forgiveness in the political sphere a more comprehensive approach is required.

When Kenyans were tortured and dehumanised in the Nyayo Chambers and detention cells it was a crime committed by the state. It was state terror. The question arises then as to who was responsible for the heinous crime: the individual officer who meted out the torture, the state agency that mandated the punishment or the one at the top, the commander in chief? If we are ever to be reconciled with our tormentor whose responsibility is it to initiate the process? How does a regime repair the damage it has done to its citizens?

When many demand justice they mostly mean retributive justice; someone must be held responsible and punished for his crime. However, retributive justice is just one form of justice, restorative and reparative justice is also the duty of the state to its citizens. Will justice be done to victims' satisfaction if those responsible for the slaughter of 3,000 in the Wagalla Massacre spend the rest of their lives in Kamiti? Is that enough?

The first step in any national healing and reconciliation process is public acknowledgment of what happened. That has not taken place in Kenya. The TJRC was an effort at uncovering the nation's ugly past and putting it on record. But its report has been denied, ignored and demeaned by successive regimes. Is it any wonder then that many cannot forgive when the state won't acknowledge the crimes committed in its name! How can you forgive when your perpetrators deny their culpability?

Why do victims have to go to court to seek reparations for the pain, suffering and torture that the government meted out on them? Should President Kenyatta not be inviting them to State House on Mashujaa Day and publicly apologise while ensuring that just reparations are made to restore them to health, prosperity and dignity? That would be real reconciliation.

This brings us back to where we started. Is the BBI designed to gloss over the past and to sanitise criminal records? Can it facilitate the recovery of stolen land and public wealth? Can it offer a new beginning by dealing effectively with a murky past? If it manages that it is a worthwhile project. If not, a waste of time and money. If we don't learn from the past, we are destined to repeat it.

(This was rejected by the Standard Media February 2020)